Tears of Theory

Creative Interventions in Global Politics

Series Editors: Shine Choi, Cristina Masters, Swati Parashar and Marysia Zalewski

The landscape of contemporary global politics is complex and oftentimes violent. Yet the urgency to provide solutions or immediate practical actions to this violence oftentimes leads to inadequate knowledge. This is despite the abundance of theoretical, conceptual and methodological tools available—much of this produced through conventional academic disciplines, notably international relations, political theory, and philosophy. But the constraints imposed on these traditional disciplines profoundly limit their ability to incorporate and make effective use of more creative and innovative methodologies found in other disciplines and genres. This series provides a unique opportunity to offer creative intellectual space to work with an eclectic and rich range of disciplines and approaches including performative methodologies, storytelling, narrative and auto-ethnography, embodied research methodologies, participant research, visual and film methodologies and arts-based methodologies.

Titles in the Series

Tears of Theory

International Relations as Storytelling

Sungju Park-Kang

ROWMAN & LITTLEFIELD
Lanham • Boulder • New York • London

Published by Rowman & Littlefield
An imprint of The Rowman & Littlefield Publishing Group, Inc.
4501 Forbes Boulevard, Suite 200, Lanham, Maryland 20706
www.rowman.com

86-90 Paul Street, London EC2A 4NE, United Kingdom

British Library Cataloguing in Publication Information Available

Library of Congress Cataloging-in-Publication Data

Names: Park-Kang, Sungju, 1977– author.
Title: Tears of theory : international relations as storytelling / Sungju Park-Kang.
Description: Lanham,, Maryland : Rowman & Littlefield, [2022] | Series: Creative
    interventions in global politics | Includes bibliographical references and index. |
    Summary: "This book talks about making storytelling and experience integral parts of
    international relations scholarship"—Provided by publisher.
Identifiers: LCCN 2021057093 (print) | LCCN 2021057094 (ebook) | ISBN
    9781538165058 (cloth) | ISBN 9781538165065 (epub)
Subjects: LCSH: International relations. | International relations—Social aspects. |
    Storytelling.
Classification: LCC JZ1242 .P38 2022 (print) | LCC JZ1242 (ebook) | DDC
    327.101—dc23
LC record available at https://lccn.loc.gov/2021057093
LC ebook record available at https://lccn.loc.gov/2021057094

This book is dedicated to
J

Contents

Foreword

When Sungju's book idea first appeared on my screen/desk, I was intrigued by the ambiguity of the title: *Tears of Theory*. My senses were asking—tearing theory? Ripping theory apart? Working with shreds of theory? Or were those fluid tears—weeping over the failures, demands and constrictions of institutionalised theory? I never asked Sungju these questions—I think I wanted to wait until I read the final manuscript. And I got to read the final draft while still in the midst of the COVID-19 pandemic, a time of pain and loss for so many. The places of privilege I inhabit have shielded me from the very worst of the pandemic, though one consequence for me of the toll of 'going on' in 'COVID-time,' had been an increasing failure to (properly) read. My scattered, darting brain, fuelled by social media 'doom scrolling,' kept inching further and further back my long-learned ability to concentrate or focus for long enough. But I had a foreword to write for Sungju's book, so I had to read Sungju's book. I opened the file on my laptop and started to read—and kept on reading, and reading. And reading. I wanted to read Sungju's book, and I began to understand more about those 'tears.'

Tears of Theory beautifully draws together stories of the personal, political, theoretical and international. It is 'simply' theory—which for me, is profound. Not a forcing of theory into and through the messy world of the personal, whether these are the everyday alleged banalities of eating lunch, paying a proofreader, finding a quiet place to think, or, day after day after day, working out how to be a better educator, which for Sungju included providing bananas for students. Bananas. One might not immediately imagine bananas as an integral part of educative experiences, though I am, unsurprisingly perhaps, reminded of Cynthia Enloe's path-breaking (or perhaps path-tearing) book *Bananas, Beaches and Bases: Making Feminist Sense of International Politics* (1989/2014). This book introduced readers to the intimate connections between the personal, local and global, including through the gendered, sexualised and racialised international marketing of bananas. I had begun teaching about gender and international relations a few years after the publication of the first edition of *Bananas*, and I recall being asked by a, somewhat perplexed, senior, white, male professor of international relations—'whatever next!?—Vegetables and IR?!' It would be hard to imagine a good contemporary IR teaching programme that did not include courses on the gendered and raced global political economies of labour and production, in which vegetables might indeed appear centre stage. As I read through Sungju's book, I felt so warmed imagining the lengthy and temporally eclectic tracks and trails of theorising global politics through and with the personal. And how what had once seemed unimaginable to write about in international relations, now so fluidly appears on the page.

Yet, these appearances on the page are too often painfully forged through struggle. As I lingered further with the book, I thought more about Sungju's references to 'someone like me'—' . . . I write this book to show that someone like me in academia can still breathe, and survive' (prologue). Also about the ruthless demands of political and academic authorities, and the price of saying 'no' to them, and I felt the tears and tears of theory more forcefully. The work of ripping and tearing at institutionally procured and vigorously defended walls around who and what can be spoken about; who and what can be written about, and even how to write—such cold, frozen forms of theory and storytelling. Though institutions can rip at, and viciously wound those who 'say no,' especially the many othered 'someones' so relentlessly frozen out. As I read Sungju's book, I keenly sensed the hurt, the pain and the struggle—the wash of tears, written and unwritten.

I think of conventional IR and the ubiquitous creation of academic *stars* emboldened by the demands of neo-liberal institutions, or rather I am drawn to unthink this and drift afar to imagine a different kind of star as I read Sungju's book. As Ocean Vuong so attentively articulates: 'Stars. Or rather, the drains of heaven—waiting. Little holes. Little centuries opening just long enough for us to slip through' (2017). Such a joyful yet paradoxical palimpsest, just like Sungju's book—all about failure and hurt but also, so importantly, about survival and the ability to transform wounds in the most luminous of ways. No wonder I kept reading.

Marysia Zalewski
Cardiff, Wales

A Letter about a Positive Curse

I may have been cursed . . . I first came up with the idea of this book in 2014. Then I had the opportunity to finish the project by 2017. But a significant delay followed—a long and complicated story. It was unexpected, and heart-breaking. Particularly since 2017, I feel I have lived with anger, although I have not usually expressed it. I could not help thinking, 'Am I cursed?'

Having survived numerous twists and turns, I decided to revise my initial project in 2019. But another substantial and unexplained delay followed. I was suffocating. Finally, a contract was secured. I then submitted a manuscript to my publisher. Due to an administrative mistake, however, the subsequent process was delayed again. That was when I said to myself, with confidence, 'I am cursed.' I did not care about the reason—the delay itself was all that mattered. Despite the various forms of delays that I faced, I managed to submit the manuscript earlier than planned. Another delay, however, struck me. I was speechless.

That was not the end. A much more complex circumstance was immediately created. Unfortunately, that process caused another delay in publication of my book. Yes, a further delay . . . I could not help wondering. 'Why does this keep happening to me?' But deep down inside, I knew that it was a mysteriously positive curse.

The chains of delays, twists and turns have consistently challenged me to think about what I really wanted. I was thankfully pushed to reflect on myself, my work and my life as a whole. In the course of this *curse*, I strongly believe that I have become a more empathetic person. I now know a bit better what it means to live without hope. I understand a bit better what it feels like to fail. I am able to be more grateful for small things than before. If I had effectively and successfully published my book as planned, I would have become rather overconfident and arrogant. So yes, I was fortunate to be cursed, if I may say so.

First and foremost, I must thank Stephen Chan and Cynthia Enloe for their incredible support for the last twelve years. Shine Choi is the one who keeps encouraging me whenever possible. And I appreciate Marysia Zalewski's generosity and thoughtfulness. Separately, my thanks extend to the Creative Interventions in Global Politics series editors. I also convey my gratitude to my mentor, Christine Sylvester.

Finland, the country of *sisu*, has become my second home. Many thanks to my colleagues and friends: Lauri Paltemaa, Outi Luova, Silja Keva, Katri Kauhanen, Anna Väre and Sabine Burghart, among others. From there, I was blessed to stay in Estonia. Thank you Elo Süld and Märt Läänemets. Finland, please do not be jealous—let me also thank Sweden, which I used to regard as my second home. There, in particular, I am grateful to Camilla Orjuela, Maria Stern, Sofie Hellberg and Gudurn 'Tibbe' Tiberg. And how can I forget Denmark? Thank you Cecilia Milwertz and Geir Helgesen. Britain, have I told you before? My heart still remains there—I am grateful to Hazel Smith, Hae-Sung Jeon, Sojin Lim, Ed Griffith, Michael Dillon and Cynthia Weber. Also, I will never forget the Netherlands—my thanks extend to Remco Breuker.

The list goes on. Your sometimes-unexpected support saved me: Annick Wibben, Laura Shepherd, Oded Löwenheim, Lene Hansen, Veronica Kitchen and the late Lily Ling. Flying to Korea, many thanks to Heejin Jung, Gwiok Kim, Sungkyung Kim, Kabwoo Koo, Soojung Lee, Wooyoung Lee, Dongchun Kim, Myungran Yi-Kim, Jiyoung Lee-An and Dean Ouellette.

Needless to say, I am grateful to my publisher and to an anonymous reviewer, in particular, for giving me courage. When my new editor Michael Kerns said, 'Nicely done,' I was moved. Many thanks to Elizabeth Von Buhr as well.

I cannot name them all for various reasons, but I would also like to thank the families of KAL 858—I may not always agree with you all, but I would support you all in one way or another.

I have never met (and probably will never meet) you in person, but my warm thanks extend to all of you: Timo Harjunpää (*Harjunpää*), Lauri Räihä (*Kaikki synnit*), Saga Norén (*Bron*), Sarah Lund (*Forbrydelsen*), Dana van Randwijck (*Noord Zuid*), Alec Hardy (*Broadchurch*), Chungho Oh (*Montage*), Hyungmin Kim (*Dark Figure of Crime*) and Soohyun Cha (*Signal*) . . . along with Frodo Baggins (*The Lord of the Rings*), Betty Anne Waters (*Conviction*), Walter Mitty (*The Secret Life of Walter Mitty*) and Father Michael Kerrigan (*Broken*).

Last, so least, I am grateful to . . . myself. Thank you, Sungju, for your perseverance, for your *sisu*.

Prologue

Everything can collapse. Even death awaits. But something must be done. Not later, right now. A door needs to be opened. Behind the door, a killer is hiding. To capture the killer, this door must be destroyed. The tool that can open the door is given to one detective. No time to hesitate. But he takes a moment, to breathe and think. Then, with a signal, he strikes. The door is broken down, colleagues enter, the killer is captured. An almost hero, the detective does not move. He is frozen, just sitting down on the ground. A worried-looking colleague tells him, 'It is over now [Se on ohi nyt].' Tears and harsh breathing engulf his body.

I was surprised by this scene from the Finnish drama/film series *Harjunpää*. That was because the detective was weeping out of fear and confusion. A fan of detective movies myself, I have never seen any lead characters weeping in such situations. It is a powerful testimony showing that a detective is also human, an individual with emotion. Timo Harjunpää is a detective in the Helsinki Police Department. He is depicted as cautious, caring and philosophical. Most importantly, however, Timo is distressed, pained and sometimes lost. Like anyone else in the real world, this detective feels and struggles.

The series is based on the novels by Matti Yrjänä Joensuu. The writer himself actually worked as a detective. This means that the work in question is entangled with the notion of experience. How is the writer's experience being used to create a story? Which part of this work is real and which part is not? To what extent does the writer employ experience to construct a societal narrative? In sum, the *Harjunpää* series could be taken as a point of departure for exploring themes such as emotion, pain and experience, in a flexible way.

In international relations (IR) and social sciences, there have been attempts to view the researcher as a detective (Keohane 1998; Thies 2002; Der Derian 2009; Park-Kang 2014). For this reason, Timo Harjunpää's situation resonated with my story. Broadly speaking, this book is about failure and hurt. More importantly, it is about survival—how to live with wounds, how to endure challenging circumstances and how to transform them into academically meaningful work, if any.

The main element in this project is concerned with my research journey of twenty years on a mysterious spy of the Cold War era. Relevant examples include among others, worries about surveillance programmes, demotivation caused by significant delays of projects, reflections on the researcher-researched relationship, critical pedagogy and punishment for pursuing a single case study. These experiences have made me better understand myself and others, particularly those who have suffered through difficult times. I believe that I have become more empathetic and humble. And I write this book to show that someone like me in academia can still breathe, and survive.

PART I

Confession

This is not the book I wanted to write.

Please let me explain. It is related to one of the main themes of the book: failure. I originally designed the book as a fiction writing project. The project aimed to explicitly employ imagination as a methodology in IR. Fictional imagination is employed to deal with lack of data and contingency surrounding it. To develop the idea, this work was supposed to present a book-length story by contextualising the case of a Korean woman spy in 1987. According to South Korea, a secret agent bombed a South Korean plane (Korean Air [KAL] flight 858) under instructions from the North Korean leadership, killing 115 people (two foreign nationals included). Subsequently, the US government designated North Korea as a state sponsor of terrorism. A film based on the official findings was later released in which the bomber was portrayed as a 'virgin terrorist.' However, many unanswered questions emerged and the families of the passengers/crews demanded a reinvestigation. These questions have resulted in two rounds of reinvestigations: first by an internal committee within the National Intelligence Service (NIS) and second by the Truth and Reconciliation Commission (TRC).

I have already published several short stories in my earlier book (Park-Kang 2014). During my PhD programme, I vaguely came up with the idea of fictional IR—employing fiction writing as a research method. When I showed my mentor a short story draft, based on my research and experience along with other people's painful lives, the mentor said that I seemed to have a talent. I did not believe it. Most of all, my first language is not English; and more importantly, because I had never written fictional stories before; I had not read a lot of fiction either. That encouragement itself was a mystery. Thankfully, with this and other unexpected support, I gradually tried (or pretended) to believe what I had not believed. Crucially, writing fiction is not about talent or some magical power. It is about how to interpret our experiences in an empathetic manner and how to translate tears into a wellspring of another possibility. I am not alone here. Lynda Barry (2008: 185), a creative writer/scholar, says that 'writing fiction is not that different from writing from your own experience.' It is my belief that I was able to write publishable short stories because those stories were drawn from my very lived experience.

Built on this publication, I wanted to develop my creative experiment into a book-length project. The previous book is written in a way that combines standard academic writing with non-standard writing. The so-called *scientific* and *literary* writings are mixed in the book. My new project aimed to offer a book-length fictional work—the whole book would have been written as a non-standard academic work. Employing fiction writing throughout the whole book should have been a significant advance in scholarship.

Unfortunately, my capability did not match it. I submitted a book proposal or a full manuscript to several publishers in turn. Responses were not entirely negative, but the key point was that my writing was not good enough to secure publication. I was disappointed but not surprised, because, after all, I was not a professional fiction writer and have had no formal training in fiction or creative writing. I had still managed to write several short stories. However, I was aware of my limit. And I had been trying to go beyond that. Or it might be the case that I had not tried hard enough. I thought I could do it somehow, until a similar question was raised during a review process managed by the current publisher. It seemed that the time had come for me to make a choice.

I spent a great deal of time reflecting on my *current* capability to offer a readable book-length fiction. I felt that I would be able to produce an acceptable manuscript for my ambitious project, provided that I had more time to work on it or get some professional training and guidance. The problem was that I would need to invest more time and a lot of energy to make it happen. Would it be worth it? I asked myself. That was because I wanted to contribute to a potential reinvestigation into the flight case as soon as I had finished the project. I strongly wanted to do something more tangible than writing. Indeed, some families of the victims and their supporters had been waiting for me in South Korea.

Therefore, I had to think hard about whether I should put my academic ambition first, or other forms of meaning and action. After very careful consideration and much thought, I decided to rearrange priorities—I chose not to pursue the fiction writing project any further, partly because I could not let those people just wait. That was how I chose to write this book. Instead of writing fiction, I decided to work on a book with non-fiction storytelling elements in it. The line between fiction and reality can be contested though (Park-Kang 2014). Here, I would like to take storytelling in the broadest possible sense: a mode of communication that allows one to make the most of one's or others' experience and the power of story in engaging with the world.

Anyway, I might come back to book-length fiction writing later, but considering my current capability, I believe that this revised effort would make my work more achievable. A storytelling or narrative project in broad terms is still challenging and unusual, at least in the field of IR. And importantly, fiction writing can also be regarded as a form of storytelling. In sum, this book is a result of compromises between my laudable plan, adjusted ambition and urgent engagement needs.

Writing this book has not been easy. One very practical challenge was related to the English language. Indeed, as a non-native speaker writing in English has been challenging throughout my career. It has been accompanied with self-doubt. 'Is my English proper? Is it grammatically correct? Can I use this expression here? Is it okay to write this way? When can I become confident in my writing?' I felt that I could not get away from these questions permanently. This uneasiness, this uncertainty has kept haunting me. At the same time, I think that not everyone, whose first language is not English, is struggling with the language issue. Maybe I am the one who is not just good enough to write in English freely? Maybe I am not talented in using a foreign language? Probably. But the thing is that I did publish my works in English. That means my English is good enough to be recognised in the world of the English language. Still, being a non-native speaker costs a lot. It takes more time, it requires more effort. Also it literally costs money if you want a professional proofreading service from a native speaker. I wished I were a native speaker. I wished my self-doubt would go away. I wished my English were perfect. I longed to be an easy-going native.

Whenever I had a writing project in English, I had an additional project in itself—to find a native speaker. I did my best to finish and polish my writing as much as I could. My writing, however, remained unfinished and unpolished until a native proofreader reviewed it. I always regarded my writing as unstable, before a native speaker had checked it. Without a native speaker, my writing was in limbo. Without a native authoriser, I could not be an author. Finding this authoriser was almost always a stressful task. Sometimes my friends authorised my writing. In return, I always gave them something as a token of gratitude—no financial element was involved though. I feared that they would take me as someone who took advantage of a friendship. Sometimes my colleagues did proofreading. In this case as well, I expressed my gratitude in various ways. But more importantly, I did not want them to see me as someone who exploited a professional relationship.

Having my friends and colleagues as potential native proofreaders, I carefully decided to contact different people each time. I tried not to ask the same person for a review consecutively. And to contact a potential reviewer, I always had to come up with another person in advance, in case the first contacted reviewer was not available. Hence, although I never intended to do so,

I ended up having a list of friends and colleagues as native English speakers who could correct my writing. I felt guilty about this all the time.

When I had an especially long text, it was difficult for me to ask my friends or colleagues—I sought help from a professional service provider. Then I would have, relatively speaking, no guilty feeling, because I paid this proofreader. In any case, my emotional labour as a non-native speaker was enormous.

But I realised that the question of language is more complicated than that. It was when I was about to publish my first book based on my PhD dissertation. The dissertation had already been proofread by a native English speaker. And some parts were revised for a book, and some parts were left unchanged. The problem occurred when a new native speaker, commissioned by a publisher, proofread a book manuscript. This new proofreader corrected various sentences which had already been reviewed by a previous proofreader, another native speaker. I thought, 'Okay, they are all native speakers, but looked at the same text differently. Who is right? Whose proofreading should I trust?'

Another uncomfortable question was raised when I found something wrong with the proofreader's correction. This native speaker's suggestion seemed to be incorrect. But I did not dare to ask the proofreader whether it was correct or not. The reason was simple—because the proofreader was a native English speaker, who was commissioned by the publisher. As a non-native speaker, I assumed that I just had to accept what the proofreader corrected. I had no authoritative voice in terms of the English language. I had had similar experiences before, when I wrote essays, journal articles and book chapters. Yes, almost whenever I had some work proofread by a native English speaker, there was something I wanted to ask. But I did not ask the questions directly. First of all, I did not want to upset the native speaker—if I make this proofreader uncomfortable, then this native speaker might not help me next time, I worried. But more importantly, I thought that I simply should trust the proofreaders in question, because they were native speakers. They have the authority that cannot be challenged by a non-native speaker, I believed.

The authority of a native speaker, however, can be very much contested by nature. Ironically, I encountered this issue when I examined my own first language, Korean. I conducted a series of interviews with the families of KAL 858 as part of my fieldwork. I recorded most of the interviews and transcribed them one by one. I tried not to miss any word from the interviews, the families' answers and my own questions. Naturally, it was a very long and painstaking process. Then an uncomfortable surprise came—my Korean language was not always correct. I, a native Korean speaker, was not using perfect Korean. This realisation led me to question the concept of the native itself. 'What does it mean to be a native speaker? Who used the term "native

speaker" first? When and why? The native . . . What does it really mean?'
Indeed, when it comes to the native Korean language, there are complicated
elements to consider. First, there is a difference between a South Korean version and a North Korean one. Secondly, within the South Korean language,
there are different dialect forms across the country. Thirdly, traditionally
speaking, the Korean language had been influenced by the languages of
neighbouring countries such as China and Japan. If so, when we talk about
the *native* Korean language, whose language is that?

Similarly, regarding the English language, there are various versions:
British, American, Canadian and Australian English, among others. Within
British English, for instance, there are differences between the English used
in London, Northern England and Scotland. So where is this native English
language? Where does it come from? When was it introduced first? By whom
and why? Is it not the case that the native language has always been in the
making? Is it not the case that the concept of the native itself is unstable? To
me, the very concept of the native became more and more problematic. My
immediate concerns remained the same though: Who should be my native
proofreader next time? And if necessary, how much should I pay?

Doing a translation presented a different kind of challenge. For example,
when I translated my interviews conducted in Korean into English, I had to be
particularly careful about wording. It was not only about the issue of the target language. Most of all, I should have asked myself. 'Did I understand the
interviewees correctly? Did I record the interviews appropriately?' To some
extent, understanding or recording the interviews itself was part of translation. It demanded a great deal of sensitivity. 'What if we did not share the
same meaning of a particular term? What if they had a different understanding of a certain concept from mine? What if my own experience or prejudice
influenced my understanding of what they said?'

A cautious mindset was required to go back and forth between my language and theirs (in that sense, reading books and articles could also be
considered as translation—not to mention materials in a foreign language).
Then, the next question was how to literally translate those Korean words into
English. I often felt like swimming in the deep ocean of languages. It was
not always easy to come up with the right English word. 'What if my choice
of this word distorted what the interviewees said? What if my understanding
of this English word was not actually correct? What if there were no exact
English equivalents?'

Sometimes I faced an ethical dilemma as a responsible researcher, and
sometimes I struggled with my capability as a non-professional translator.
Moreover, when my English translation was corrected by a native speaker,
I had to go through the whole process again. I tried to preserve the original
intention and meaning of the interviews, but at the same time, I was often

forced to make a compromise for practical purposes. The lesson I learnt? To do a translation is a constant negotiation—languages and meanings are endlessly flying around, and you need to picture the most appropriate expression in your own time.

As a non-native speaker, however, writing in English was my main concern. Let's go back to the question of proofreaders' corrections. There were several recommendations that seemed to be problematic. But I was not sure about my concerns as my first language was not English. I got confused, as my belief in the authority of a native speaker collapsed. The story did not end there. Another problem with the correction was that deleted or replaced words seemed to generate (sometimes totally) different meanings. For instance, my original wording was 'She almost cried,' and this was changed into 'She cried'—that is, the word 'almost' was deleted. What I intended to say was that she looked very sad so that she could cry, but actually she did not. According to the correction, however, she did cry—the subtle emotional state was erased. My acknowledgements section had a problem as well. This section was written in the form of a letter, where I used the word 'you' referring to all the people I had mentioned. It was my strategic choice of writing. But in the native speaker's proof pages, the word was replaced with 'he' or 'she'; in some cases, the gender of people was changed. The native speaker's standard grammar overruled my flexible and creative element in my writing.

All of this led me to wonder: To what extent is the native speaker's proofreading authoritative? To what extent can non-native speakers write in English? More fundamentally, to what extent can non-native speakers' works be original? Where is an author? Where is a proofreader? And where is the line between them? Meanwhile, it was important to realise that my questions and doubts were not unique to English writing. Going back to the issue of my own native language, I also made mistakes when I published books and articles in Korean. As a native Korean speaker, I knew that my Korean was not perfect—my language had to be checked by a professional native Korean proofreader. And some of this proofreader's corrections were corrected again by me. If so, it might be wise to accept that our language itself, our writing itself, whether it is in English or any other language, cannot exist as a one-off project. Language and writing exist as a process. There is no perfect (native) language user. In that sense, all writing is not alright.

There is still another question that I have hardly asked before, a quite simple and basic one. As a multilingual person, who is now able to speak several European languages, I can finally ask the question myself. 'Why on earth do I have to write in English?' It is a somewhat foolish question. But indeed, why English? I could have done all my writings in Korean (it would have been much easier) or I could have published my works in other languages (if I had a chance and capability). Of course, if you are in an institution or a country where the working language is English, it becomes a different matter. But the key question is, why are researchers actively encouraged or pushed to publish in English? 'That's because . . . English is a dominant language?' Yes, no one could easily deny the hegemonic status of the English language in academic communities. And obviously, this is not limited to the scholarly world in this age of so-called globalisation. To keep one's position in academia or to secure tenures, to survive as a scholar, you are almost required to write in English. Hence, native English speakers have privileges. They, for example, do not necessarily have to think about all the questions that I had. Working with those questions is laborious. And the privileged sometimes do not even realise that they are privileged.

I now begin to think that I do not wish to be a native English speaker. If I had been a native speaker, I would not have had to spend time on bothering myself with all those uneasy questions. I felt, however, that I have gained some insights thanks to that laborious work. Although it would still be inconvenient and costly, I would rather like to remain as a non-native speaker—a unique and diligent speaker.

Combinations

Based on my (non-individually owned) experience/research or stories above, I would like to talk about tears of theory—a theory full of tears, a theory out of tears or a theory that is crying. Here, I take the notion of theory in the broadest possible terms. Starting with the title, *Tears of Theory*, a theory can be taken as something in conventional academic terms—a proposition or a set of ideas to explain things, aiming to establish universal principles. Or it can be taken as scholarly works in general, one's academic achievements. What I want to suggest is that a theory comes from our body—it comes from our experience and life. A theory or knowledge is situated in a certain time and space.

Another meaning of theory in this context is related to the case of KAL 858. Due to its mysterious nature, the case has generated a lot of theories— a theory here means an idea employed to account for a certain situation, particularly when that situation potentially involves a high degree of contingency. For instance, there are several family members of KAL 858 who strongly believe that the case was an inside job of the South Korean military government. Some people and the government just ignore this idea as a mere conspiracy theory; others take it seriously.

Whatever the case, I would say that people need to understand *why* this theory has been present for so long—the official and dominant narrative of the case of KAL 858 is almost completely based on the words of the self-confessed bomber Hyunhee Kim, not evidence. The family members have not seen the dead bodies of their loved ones; there is no proper wreckage of the flight; the bomber's statements contain numerous contradictions. Therefore, is it still appropriate to simply dismiss the so-called conspiracy theory? This theory comes from pain, or tears of ordinary people who have been forced to accept the government's problematic investigation result. Again, the theory here is drawn from people's body, pain and emotions. Whether this theory is proved to be true is another matter.

PART II

Enigma

I was first engulfed by a Cold War mystery as an undergraduate student. I participated in a national thesis competition organised by the South Korean Ministry of Unification, a specialised ministry dealing with inter-Korean affairs. Based on the unanswered questions cast by reinvestigation campaigners, part of my thesis questioned the official account of the case of KAL 858. The thesis won an award, but it was withdrawn because of that challenge. Ever since I went through the case of the unification thesis, as I call it, I had been worried about surveillance.

Back then (and still), I could not understand why the Ministry of Unification had suddenly changed its decision. They selected my thesis as the second best and the award ceremony was only five days away. This prize was decided through a multi-stage evaluation process. First, internal committee members chose a number of theses. Those works were then reviewed and shortlisted by external experts. Then, finalists were selected and awarded prizes accordingly. If there were serious problems with my thesis, the work should have been eliminated at the early stage. But only right before the award ceremony, they asked me to revise the thesis. That was so late. They even said, 'If you don't have time to revise, we could do it instead . . . on behalf of you.' That was an extremely unusual and kind (?) offer.

Most likely they may have thought that I would just follow their request. At the end of the day, this prize would give me money along with an honour issued by the government, a privileged position as a future academic. Particularly for young college students like me, this would be *the* great recognition. How wonderful. Who could resist such things? Well . . . They got me wrong.

Rejecting the government's demand was actually easy, quite straightforward. I did not have to think much, because the demand itself was simply unjust. It violated academic freedom; it suppressed freedom of expression; it crushed freedom of conscience. Most of all, I thought that the unanswered questions about the case of KAL 858 raised by various people were still valid. So I said *no* to the government. It was a natural answer indeed. But the price I had to pay afterwards was another thing. Given this rather sensitive nature of the event, I struggled to figure out how such a scandal could happen. As the case of KAL 858 had a lot to do with the intelligence agency, I suspected that the NIS may have intervened. I felt like I was being watched by someone, or something. I started avoiding people. When I had to go out for lunch, I chose a place that had fewer people. When I walked on a street, I sometimes looked behind me. I tried not to talk. I could not eat well. I also had sleep problems. Furthermore, I was not able to concentrate during class—my head was full of various suspicions. 'Why is this happening? Whose idea is this? Who should I trust? What am I supposed to do?' It seemed like everything was unreal. This sort of thing should happen only in movies. My world was collapsing. A huge wave of confusion landed on me.

Two years later, I found myself working with the families of KAL 858. Those families had been campaigning for the reinvestigation of the case, as there were many questions surrounding what really happened. I learnt that these families used to be under surveillance by the intelligence agency. That was when I could revisit my own case of the unification thesis from a different perspective. That fear, that confusion and that anger . . . I now began to think of my experience as a bridging point between those families and myself. Of course, my own case was so trivial compared to that of the families. But still, I came to realise that there must be a bigger picture there in my experience.

At the same time, I became more careful when it came to my everyday life. There was a good reason. The families, their supporters and I met regularly to discuss the campaign. At least on two occasions, the meeting abruptly ended as we sensed that someone was following and watching us. I did not feel safe enough at my school either. I was working on an MA project on the case of KAL 858. My original project dealt with a very different subject. Having started seeing those families, however, I changed my plan. The decision was not so easy. Due to this change, I even had to delay my graduation. But deep down, I knew that I wanted to work on this subject.

You may call it destiny if you like. Indeed, going back to the unification thesis case, I wanted to forget all of it—everything about the prize and every-thing about KAL. Why? Because it made me extremely uncomfortable. I did not want any more confusion. I feared chaos. One should never study things like this in Korea, I thought. In October 2002, however, twists and turns came. Yes, that destined evening when a mysterious thing happened to me—a nervous breakdown following the thesis case. My mother was so worried that she brought a doctor home. The doctor checked me and said, 'Your heart is full of heat.' I subsequently took some medicines. While resting, I became convinced that I had done nothing wrong. It was the government that had made things complicated. I did not want to be silenced. I brought the thesis case to the National Human Rights Commission. Going further, I went to a graduate school to study inter-Korean relations. I still hesitated to do something directly about the KAL case though.

In 2003, I decided to attend a press conference organised by the Families and the Civil Truth Campaigns for KAL 858. I had a busy schedule that day and took a taxi to arrive on time. When I got out, I felt something was strange—I left my file case in the taxi. There were important documents, some of which were to be delivered to the families of KAL. I turned back and frantically chased after the taxi. But it was too late. My documents were gone and my mind went blank. Consequently, I could not go to the meeting. 'This might be . . . a warning. I should forget KAL 858.'

Life is a mystery. At last, I met the families of KAL the following year. Since then, I had attended almost all the meetings and activities arranged by them over the next few years. But again, I worried about surveillance. For example, the balloon affair as I call it. One day when I got back from the school, there was a balloon in front of my home. What did I do? I stepped back and looked around me. I fetched a long stick then hid myself behind the wall. I almost covered my eyes with one hand. And now, I slowly and very carefully touched the balloon with the stick. Well . . . I suspected that the balloon could be a bomb or something. People would laugh at this. I was overreacting.

But I had every reason to be cautious. That was particularly the case in the sense that my graduate school was a specialised education institute—the only graduate institution in the country in which whole programmes focus on North Korea and inter-Korean relations. Naturally there were many people from the intelligence agency, military, police and other government organisations. Full-time students like me were rare. Obviously I kept a careful watch on, most of all, students from the NIS. It was an open secret that they used a code name when they formally referred to their agency—the Century Culture Company. Some full-time students of this school were often hired by the NIS upon their graduation. Before I came to this school, I was not aware enough of this rather sensitive element. But I could not do anything about that. The only thing I could do was to keep a watch on them or to avoid them as much as I could.

There was one person who especially troubled me. A middle-aged man, who wore glasses and almost all the time kept an impassive face. I gave my own code name to this person: the Away One. The Away One's background was a bit unclear. It seemed he had worked for the government-owned media before. That was all I knew. Unlike other part-time students who came to the school in the evening after their work, the Away One stayed in the school mostly all day. So I came across him here and there. When the Away One saw me, a mysterious smile appeared on his poker face. I did not like that smile—I slightly bowed to the Away One and went away. For some reason, the Away One approached me several times. 'Mr Sungju Park-Kang, can we have a chat?' That was very alarming. 'Well . . . I have something to do.' I bowed, then went away. Of course it was possible that the Away One was just a normal person. But my radar always made a beeping sound when the Away One was there. I did everything to keep away from the Away One.

Then, the Away One made a rather aggressive move. That was one of those moments when I bumped into the Away One. In an empty corridor of the school the Away One said. 'Mr Sungju Park-Kang, can I talk to you?' I slightly bowed as usual, and just went my way. 'Hey! Sungju Park-Kang!' the Away One shouted. I stopped but did not look behind me. I could feel tension though. 'I said, I want to talk to you!' shouted the Away One again. His voice was filled with a bit of anger. I now turned around. The mysterious face was staring at me. Without words, I bowed . . . and went away.

Back to my seat in the study room, I closed my eyes. I took a deep breath. I stood up and went back to that corridor. I then headed to a lecture room where the Away One was sitting alone. 'Knock, knock.' I entered the room. 'Excuse me, but may I ask you something please?' That was the first time I talked to the Away One. 'Yes,' nodded the Away One. I looked him straight in the eye, and asked. 'Do you work for the NIS?' ' . . . ' The Away One closed his eyes. I waited patiently. 'No . . . ' said the Away One. I kept looking him in the eye. 'I don't work for the NIS. I may look like it, but . . . I'm not that kind of person as you think.' I still looked straight in his eyes. 'I wanted to get along with full-time students. I just wanted to get to know you.' A quiet, but tense moment. 'Yeah . . . I see,' I said. Still sitting, the Away One now stared at me. That apathetic face began to penetrate into my eyes. 'Thank you . . . ' I bowed, and left. That was how the first ever and last conversation between the Away One and me went. I thought that was it.

But the Away One never went away. Sometime later, he came to the study room where full-time students were staying. He just did not stop by, but now had his place there—two seats away from me. How did he get that seat? We do not know. But clearly, my radar made a huge beeping sound. When I was sitting or working there, I could not stop feeling that the Away One was watching. And I worried that the Away One might do something while I was away—for example, looking around my desk, checking my computer or things like that. The Away One now spent much time together with me and my classmates. When I went out for lunch with my friends in the study room, the Away One joined us. After lunch, I had a digestive problem. When I played *jokgu* (football tennis) with my friends, the Away One joined us. During the game, I could not focus on the ball. The Away One was almost always around me.

Feeling constantly watched, I decided to take some action. It was another usual day that the Away One was sitting not far away from me. The Away One was not working there—he was just sitting, slightly leaning his body towards me. Here, an adverb must be stressed. Yes, not directly but slightly. Although there were separate desks with small walls, from the Away One's position I was easily seen. I waited until the Away One left. He seemed to go home or somewhere else. Other people left as well. I walked towards the Away One's desk. Nothing much was there. I stepped back and opened the study room's door, looking left and right. No one seemed to come and I closed the door. I then began to examine the Away One's desk from top to bottom, like a detective inspecting a crime scene.

Part of myself hoped not to find anything suspicious. Like the balloon affair, nothing should come out. It did not take long before my hope was crushed. 'What is this . . . ?' Around the upper part of the desk, something was shining. It looked like a thin plastic—a plastic sheet, which was similar to a mirror. Its direction was important. Out of curiosity I sat on a chair, then looked at it. The mirror-like plastic was . . . reflecting my seat.

Another person that troubled me was actually from the intelligence agency. Yes, indeed. As a middle-aged man with a deep voice, he appeared to be friendly. He had graduated from the best university in the country and had been working for the NIS for many years. I bumped into him frequently at the school library. Most of the time he was using a copy machine there. That he was working for the NIS itself was alarming enough to invite caution and distance. I made up a code name for this person as well: the Away Two. What alarmed me most was that the Away Two was always there when I visited the school while studying and working abroad. I left the school for the UK and the Away Two would still bump into me over the next eight years or so. As I did not have a place in the study room anymore, I just stayed in the library. In other words, I was seen by the Away Two on a regular basis. It is a bit strange . . . I thought whenever I bumped into the Away Two.

If it had been one or two times, I would have just thought, what a coincidence. But if it became a rule over the eight years without exception, that was a different story. In that particular place and in that particular time, the Away Two was always there, as if he were waiting for me. Was it a pure coincidence? Well, maybe . . . But remember—he was (and is?) working for the NIS. My fellow student in the year above had been very active, from the government's perspective, in her leftist social movement. This fellow student once said to me and my friends. 'He [the Away Two] told me that I am on the NIS watch-list in which I am classified as a person of interest.' To believe or not, something like that. To put it differently, the Away Two may have had a link to the NIS surveillance system in one way or another. That was why my radar made a huge beeping sound when the Away Two approached and talked to me. 'Ah, long time no see. How have you been? Are you still in the

UK?' 'Well, I have moved to another country.' 'Why?' 'Ah . . . to take up my new position?' 'Oh really? That's good, and . . . please give me your business card.' 'Well . . . I didn't make a card.'

One other person on my watch-list was my fellow student in the year below. A relatively young and very masculine man. His unexpected (but somewhat understandable) move raised my eyebrows—probably long before or upon his graduation, he had been preparing to enter the intelligence agency. He revealed the news to me and other students while he was working on a final selection stage. Yes, he had passed several stages already and was about to be hired by the NIS. At that very moment when he delivered the news, I made up a code name for him: the Away Three.

When I had a farewell gathering before I left for the UK, the Away Three gave me a present. It was a USB memory stick. 'Ah . . . thank you,' I said. Actually, I was not thankful at all. First, I was not very pleased that the Away Three wanted to work for the NIS. Related to this, furthermore, the USB stick became something that should be handled with caution. 'This could be used for surveillance,' I suspected. If other people who I had trusted gave this USB, I would not have thought like that. But because it was the Away Three, I needed to be away from this. I still wanted to trust him though. That was why I did not throw away the USB—I kept it while I was in the UK. Nonetheless, I had never used it; I did not even open its wrapping. Sometime later, I heard that the Away Three failed to get a job at the NIS. But oddly, just like the Away Two, he was always there at the school when I stopped by the library—not once or twice, but every time. Another pure coincidence? Before I left the UK for another country, I visited a small lake. The Away Three's USB present flew from my hand, then dived into the water.

My radar had to operate constantly and vigorously. Indeed, a person from the intelligence agency even came to the school to see me. It was when I published an article in which I strongly criticised the NIS committee for not conducting a thorough reinvestigation into the case of KAL 858. One day, I went outside and got back to the school. My fellow student told me. 'Someone from the NIS came to see you.' It turned out that a full-time student who landed a job at the NIS after her graduation wanted to talk to me. Her name was familiar. Although I had not met her before, I heard about this person several times from my teachers and fellow students in the year above.

Why did she want to see me? No one knew. What I knew was that there was a real possibility of the NIS surveillance on me. A human rights lawyer, representing the families of KAL 858, once warned me. I came briefly back to Korea for my fieldwork and met this lawyer. We had known each other since I got involved in the campaigns organised by the families of KAL. While we were eating at a restaurant, the lawyer suddenly asked me. 'Uhmm . . . let me see. Look, over there . . . Was he already here before we came, or did he come after we sat here?' A seemingly middle-aged man was reading a newspaper. 'Well . . . I am not sure. But why do you ask?' The lawyer answered in a serious tone of voice. 'Look Sungju. You should be aware that someone like you quite possibly has been on the NIS watch-list. I can safely say that . . . ' Yes, my radar had a reason to be turned on . . . always.

But I am human after all—I could get other people wrong. There was one student several years below, who came to 'admire' me. According to him, he was really impressed by my book based on the MA thesis—of course, it was about the case of KAL 858. We happened to meet together when I briefly came back to Korea. He was in China continuing his study, but briefly got back to Korea as well. So we encountered each other at the school. Since then, we exchanged emails several times over the next four or five years. Usually he first contacted me each year. He wanted to know what I was doing, where I was working and so on. I responded in a friendly manner, sometimes with a long message.

But at some point, I began to think a bit cautiously. It was when the email ended with this note: 'I'd very much like to know how you are doing, what you are thinking. I'd like to know very often, indeed.' Now I became curious: 'Why does he keep contacting me? Why is he still in China? Why does he want to know this and that? Why . . . ?' A mixed feeling slowly surrounded me. Then my radar made a beeping sound . . . quietly. I sighed, and decided not to respond. About three months later, I felt sorry. I might have misunderstood him . . . Feeling guilty I belatedly sent a reply. That was the last correspondence we exchanged. I have not heard from him since. I still do not know why.

I was aware that I would keep living with this cautious or sometimes anxious attitude and mixed feeling as long as I work on the case of KAL 858. I would constantly face uncertainty as long as I work with those families. I myself often wonder what has sustained me for the last twenty years. I do not have an easy answer. I have tried to follow my inner voice and here I am. I still remember the moment when the government launched its historic reinvestigation of the case in 2005. Three years prior in 2002, the government cancelled my thesis award because I insisted that the case needed to be reinvestigated. I somehow felt that I had done the right thing. But a sense of uncertainty did not go away. In December that year, I finished the MA project. It was the first ever thesis on the case of KAL 858. I could not believe that I had completed it. I had survived a troubling and confusing time. I often worried that someone or something could do harm to me—to prevent me finishing the thesis. Yes I did, until the very last moment.

When I was waiting for the copies of my bounded thesis, something seemed to be wrong. Although an arranged delivery time passed, a representative of the printing and binding company did not turn up. I used this company's service several times earlier, but the representative was never late. I called his phone, but could not reach him. 'What happened? By any chance . . . did someone . . . ?' Several hours later, I breathed a sigh of relief. The representative came with the copies of the thesis. He said that he had a car accident, which was fortunately not so serious. So, there was a little drama until the end.

Such drama continued while I was working on my PhD thesis. One day in summer, I made an important decision. I heard and read a lot about the NIS, a spy agency; I attended several press conferences or demonstrations in front of the agency. But I had never got into the place before. And now, it was time. To file a Freedom of Information Act (FOIA) request, I decided to visit the agency. I hesitated long before I made this decision. The NIS has been accused of covering up the case for a long time. It was fair to assume that the intelligence agency might regard someone seeking to obtain the documents as a threat to them. Besides, unlike other countries, in South Korea one must provide a national identification number and other personal information to obtain secret documents (the system changed in 2021). Someday they might use my information against me, I thought.

Nevertheless, I wanted to file the request. More than that, I was willing to do so in person. Why? I remembered what Molly Andrews (2007: 44) said in *Shaping History: Narratives of Political Change*: 'If we do not feel ourselves to be personally at risk when we interrogate the lives of others, then we are not doing our jobs.'

Right . . . but wait. If you think of MI5 the Security Service or MI6 the Secret Intelligence Service, please forget it. Unlike MI5 or MI6, which can be reached comfortably in central London, the NIS seems to want to play hide-and-seek. It is located in a remote and mountainous area outside Seoul. It is not easy to get there by public transportation. The agency is surrounded by hills and woods. Once you arrive in the vicinity of the agency, a wide and relatively long way decorated by yellow-black barricades would welcome you. Only after you digest this yellow-black greeting, you can reach the main entrance. See? Forget MI5 and MI6, whose locations and doors are easy to find—compared to the NIS, they even look as friendly as your neighbour's house.

That day, I went into the office of civil affairs right next to the main entrance. Naturally I became a bit nervous. I was not a big fan of CCTV, so as I was inside the spy agency, I tried to hide myself to avoid being filmed directly—just small things like lowering my head, or keeping my distance from cameras as much as possible. Of course, I did not think it would help me much. But that was my way of passive resistance, if you like.

Once my request was registered, I asked. 'Can I have a receipt or something like that?' 'Well . . . We do not issue such a thing.' 'Ah . . . But if you make this sort of application in other organisations, you would get one.' 'Yes, but this is the intelligence agency. We are different.' 'Excuse me, but . . . ' I hesitated. I did not want to argue with the NIS staff. But I could not just give up. 'I am sorry to bother you, but how . . . then how can I prove that I made the request today and you received it?' 'We will get in touch with you sir. Hope you understand.' I quickly stared around the office, and left.

On my way back, I decided to take a taxi hoping to be away from the place as soon as possible. When one taxi was coming closer to me, I could notice another taxi suddenly rushing into me. I could not move, because everything was happening so quickly. 'Screeeeeech!!' The unpleasant noise was generated by an urgent brake. The two cars were close enough to clash almost. 'F***!! Are you crazy!?' The driver of the first taxi shouted. The second taxi driver bowed, then left. Skid marks as clear as the yellow-black barricade testified the dangerous moment. A strong burning rubber smell filled the road. Was it just a fortunate (?) incident? Was it a wicked attempt to harm me? Or something else? One thing was clear though. The NIS rejected my request for information.

Surely, my radar cannot be perfect. I myself am fully aware of that. What is important is that the radar should be always in operation. For a while this radar has not made any beeping sound. That was a good sign. But because it has been so quiet, I wondered whether my radar has stopped working at all. Well, I was mistaken. When I first started to work as assistant professor, I attended a big North Korea-related international conference. At the evening reception I had the opportunity to talk to some of the speakers. They were all North Korean defectors. When I was about to leave, someone called my name. 'Mr Sungju Park-Kang?' Then suddenly . . . my radar made a sound. Long time, no hear! I was immediately alarmed. Given the voice and accent, this person was obviously a middle-aged man from (South) Korea. First, during my stay in Europe for many years, I had never met Koreans calling me by my full name with that title. I met very few Korean people though. Secondly, therefore, I had a reason to believe that this particular person already got some information about me. The question was, why and how?

I turned around. The man briefly introduced himself. 'I'm sorry, but I was leaving. Have a good evening,' I said and quickly left. I went directly to my office and turned on my computer. I typed the man's name with some key words in the search box. After several attempts, I came to learn that this man was from the NIS-affiliated institute in Korea. With further investigation, I was able to identify that this man had worked at the NIS for decades and retired. It appeared that he had moved to the institute upon his retirement. And he was staying in the same university as me, hopefully by chance . . . Long live the radar.

Of course, everything could be a coincidence. If so, that might be the core of fear of surveillance. Minding itself controls you—it censors your behaviour; it governs your thought. Most of all, however, you limit yourself. Again, let me go back to my fieldwork in Korea while I was working on the PhD project. As always, except my mother and one close friend, I did not let other people know my visit. When I arrived in Korea and called my mother, she said, 'You need to go to the local government building. There is a letter addressed to you.' It was about my military training as a reservist. I had already finished all the regular trainings over six years or so; sometimes I was punished as a conscientious objector, but in the end I attended every required session. Members of the Reserve Forces however are still required to go to a temporary training when the authority calls them. If they cannot attend the training, they should notify the relevant bodies, which demands some paperwork.

'Of all days . . . why now?' I did not have any choice. My mother and I agreed to meet at the local government building. One minor issue was that my family had moved to another city while I was abroad. In other words, I was not so familiar with this new city. And I did not have much time either. So I decided to take a taxi from the train station. 'Welcome.' 'To the local government building please.' The taxi started to move. The new city was almost like a country area. 'Here we are.' 'Okay.' I thanked the driver and the taxi left. But something was strange . . . It was not the government building. There was a big building, but it was not the right place.

I did not know what to say, I did not know what to do. I tried to be calm. First of all, I thought about my mother. She was waiting for me. I did not have a mobile phone and could not see a public phone either. So I had to hurry. But the problem was how to find the local government building. I walked around here and there. Now, I decided to take a taxi again. It was not easy though. I did not know where I was; I could not see any taxi and mysteriously, I could not see many people either. Finally, I managed to get in a taxi. 'To the local government building please. I am already quite late. Could you go faster please?'

What happened next left me puzzled. This taxi headed back in the direction that the previous taxi drove. The government building was located in the opposite direction. I finally arrived at the building almost one hour late, and my radar made a beeping sound. 'Something seems to be going on here.' My mother was waiting for me on the ground floor. As soon as I saw her, I stared around the place quickly. We might be being watched now, I thought. Taking a cautious measure, I suggested going upstairs. But I did not say why. My mother reluctantly followed me. Now on the first floor, I explained why I was so late. And I had some usual conversation with her—how I had been and so on. I then suggested coming back to the ground floor, where my paperwork needed to be done. Reluctantly, my mother followed me again. Well, everything on that day still remains a mystery. Why did the taxi driver drop me off in the wrong place? How was the training day arranged in such a way? There was one thing I realised though—I was censoring myself.

Encounters

11 March 2009, Busan Exhibition and Convention Center. Hyunhee Kim, wearing a black suit, walked towards the building where her press conference would take place. There was a heavy security presence. First, two lines of a human wall were formed to make an exclusive way for Kim. Surrounded by that human wall, she was guarded and followed by at least three members of Police Special Forces. Inside the building Kim and a young Japanese Koichiro Iizuka, the son of Yayeko Taguchi, approached the entrance of the press conference hall. They walked arm in arm while smiling. An old man Shigeo Iizuka, the brother of Taguchi, followed them. Once they entered the hall, however, with camera flashes all around, Kim stopped smiling whereas the young man did not. 'Today . . . well . . . I met the son . . . and family of Ms Yayeko Taguchi, who taught me Japanese in North Korea . . . it's really, in fact . . . I haven't slept well for the last couple of nights. I was so happy . . . and it also reminded me of my mother. I was too touched to get sleep', said Kim in a voice shaking with emotion (Nocut TV 2009). 'What I'd like to say clearly is that this case of KAL . . . is a terror attack done by North Korea, and that I am not a fake anymore,' Kim said in a decisive voice.

'In December 1997, I . . . gave my book royalties to the families of the deceased when we met. At that time . . . we cried a lot together, and I was told to live a good life. But . . . after that, during the former government, some of the families raised questions. Of course, most of the families of the deceased all acknowledge that the case of KAL was committed by North Korea,' she hastened to add. 'Some of the families still say things like, there is no evidence of North Korea's bombing whatsoever . . . well . . . although twenty years have already passed, it is very sad that they don't know who did it,' said Kim as if it was such a shame. 'So considering the nature of today's meeting, I don't want to say things like this, but as for me . . . if the families of the deceased acknowledge that the case of KAL was a terror case perpetuated by North Korea, and if there is no other different purpose then I would be able to accommodate their demand for the meeting.'

One reporter asked about a famous flower-girl photo, which was presented as evidence showing that she was from North Korea. 'The issue of the photo of the flower-girl has already, clearly been settled. I first testified that I went there as a flower-girl at that time and later in the course of checking a couple of photos . . . in fact, within that photo, the first one which was said to be like I was not there, actually I was there. I was covered . . . by the person in front of me, so I was not shown. Because all this was later confirmed, today in this place where I meet the family of Yayeko Taguchi . . . ' said Kim with an uneasy look on her face. 'It would be courteous for you to avoid that issue, I think.' When it came to her claim that she was persecuted during the last govern-ment: 'As you all may know, well . . . during the former government, such thing happened . . . ' she paused. 'Well, I don't want to go into detail today. As the current government is investigating the things that occurred during the last government . . . I am now waiting for the result of the investigation,' Kim said in a seemingly moderate tone of voice.

* * *

'To save my soul,' I whispered. I finally decided to leave. Why? 'To do what I want, to save my soul,' I repeated. It was a sad conclusion, but I was convinced that this should be a happy resignation from my role as assistant professor. The only way to save my soul was to quit.

I was so pleased to get my first job several years ago. Becoming a univer-sity professor meant a lot. When I broke the news to my mother by phone, there was a long emotional silence—she just cried. I could not say anything either. Only tears dropped. 'My dear son, your dream has come true.' Well, my dream was not to become a professor, but to become a *scholar*. But obvi-ously, it was a great deal to start to work as an established member of the aca-demic community. Back in my home country, traditionally speaking, teachers or professors are highly respected. After the phone call, I graciously kissed my phone. 'The title doesn't matter to me. I'm just glad to get a job . . . just grateful.' Indeed, I did not care about specifics—let's say, salary. I was just honoured and deeply happy. I then took another job, again as a lecturer (assis-tant professor) here in the UK. That was how it started.

'I am sorry that you had to see all this.' 'Oh, that's okay . . . ' I said. There was a staff meeting at our office, where four lecturers were staying. Yes, four peo-ple in the same room. This was the first surprise I had when I started working here. Even when I was a PhD student a shared office for only two people was provided. But now, as a lecturer or assistant professor I was crammed into this four-person space. No privacy, not enough bookshelves, no quiet research time, no confidential meetings with students. Everyone was squeezed.

Technically speaking, it was already my second office. Before my arrival, I happened to find out that there would be no single office for me. It later turned out that most staff members here did not have their own space. When I asked how many people would be sharing the office, the answer was four, myself included. From the very beginning, I knew that there was something strange. I then requested the relevant parties to check whether there could be another space for me—not a single office, given the circumstances, but a bit better place than a shared one for four. Upon my arrival, I was directed to the current place: this shared space for four, but in practice for three people as one lecturer had moved to another building. Still, there were four desks and it looked a bit crowded already. But this was the best option the University could offer me; and it turned out that the originally suggested office was much smaller than this one, which means I could have ended up being in an incredibly compact office, far worse than the current one. So I decided to just accept it.

For some reason, there were no proper bookcases in the office. Only a few small bookshelves, a single flat surface above the desk. They were not enough for four people. I alone had about ten big boxes full of books, documents and other stuff already. 'What should I do?' I wondered. I looked around the whole space, and sighed. I just decided to put the boxes around the desk, with books and documents still inside. I did not have my own office phone either. I expected that everything would be ready for me to start working immediately. That was what I asked several times to the university administration, particularly given that I had arrived very late due to the visa issue. Indeed, I even asked whether I could get my staff account to access the intranet, which would allow me to familiarise myself with the overall school system, including class timetables and so on. Unfortunately it did not work out. And here I was. Just one day before my very first session. I cleaned the desk and sat down on a chair. Quite a rough start. But I said to myself. 'Well, at least I have a space here. I am still grateful that I got this job.'

In that shared office, there was almost no privacy. For instance, after teaching, I just wanted to rest quietly. But there was always something going on there—other teachers' students coming and going, the telephone or mobile phone ringing, various colleagues to meet other officemates, etc. I always brought my own lunch box, but I would not dare to have meals in the office as I did not want to disturb my officemates. To make matters worse, there was no dining table or enough space for people to eat in the common kitchen. I did not know where to go. It was one of those days when I finished my class and wanted to be alone. It was like I was being suffocated. So I just went outside, and began to walk. I reached the city centre which was about a twenty-minute walk from the office. I stopped by a supermarket and grabbed a sandwich. Outside the store, I began to eat. I looked at the street. A lot of people moving around. Not peaceful, no. I looked up to the sky. Blue and almost clear, with very few clouds. This sky seemed to give me a little comfort.

'Sir, sir.' I heard something. 'Sir, please sir.' There was a beggar, a man with a frowning face showing hands. Clearly this man wanted some money. 'Sir, sir.' I said nothing. I felt sympathetic, of course. To be honest, however, I felt invaded. I felt that my rarely-found-small-peace was interrupted. That was a big deal. I just stared blankly at the man. 'Please sir, please.' The man kept holding out his hands. Suddenly I got enraged. 'Oh, please!' I shouted. The man looked perplexed. I felt sorry, and tried to apologise. At that moment, the man was approached by someone who kindly gave him a coin. I felt awful; I had become a horrible person. My very brief moment of peace was destroyed, and replaced with regret. Normally, I would not have behaved like that. No, not particularly to a person who wanted some mercy and care . . . how mean. Since I had moved, something was changing inside me, uncomfortably. I looked at the sky again. 'I want myself back. I want my own place. I need somewhere I can be alone.'

I returned to the office building. I was determined to find some quiet place. There must be some space. And yes, there was. I managed to find a small place, with a door sign of a white cross on a green background—a first aid kit symbol. The room was supposed to be used for people who felt sick and needed some medical attention. I realised that this room was very often empty. There was a bed, something that one could find in a hospital. Probably this could serve, for example, as an alternative dining table? I did not feel entirely good, but this room became my secret garden. Whenever I used this room, I locked the door. There was no window, no dining table. But I could breathe and eat peacefully. I still felt guilty about using the room for another purpose. And I was careful not to lose this little moment of peace. Before entering and leaving the room, I put my ear to the door to detect any sound from outside. Only when I caught no sound, only when I was sure that no one was out there, I came in and went out. That way, this seemingly secret garden became the only place where I could find peace.

One month later, a nice surprise there. The Department, in some mysterious way, decided to provide me with a single office. Such a surprise, because I had not asked for it. I had not even complained about anything. The thing is that there was an empty space which was reserved for medical reasons. According to regulations, when a member of staff needs a single office for health reasons, if they have a disability or the like, this member is entitled to use the space alone. Strictly speaking, my case did not count here. But my Head of Department made a suggestion to the relevant administration party and it was approved. A very generous and thoughtful measure indeed. Maybe my grateful mindset had paid off. Maybe the Head of Department felt sorry for me—I had arrived one day before the first class, I shared the office where heavy student traffic took place, I was surrounded by a number of boxes unpacked. But strangely enough, I felt a bit guilty. Knowing that most of my colleagues were still sharing the office with each other, I did not feel comfortable. And that was why I did not put a name tag on my office door. I did not want other people to know that I was using a single space. I got my own desperately wanted office, although I had not done anything at all. I should be happy. I was, however, sorry. Finding peace did not make me feel peaceful.

My new office was small. And there was not much furniture. For instance, a bookcase was missing. The Head of Department suggested that I could at least have a bookcase. I was grateful, but politely declined it. 'I think I am already privileged as I use a single office. I mean most other colleagues use a shared office. So you know, I'm okay . . . ' 'Are you sure?' 'Yes, really. I'm just grateful for having this space. That's all.' 'Well, if you say so . . . ' 'Yes, I mean it. But thank you for asking.' Indeed, with my own office, I now felt everything began to go much more smoothly. Although I was still surrounded by several boxes, without a bookcase, I gladly embraced it. After two consecutive classes, I could get some rest quietly. When lunch time came, I did not have to worry about where to eat. When there were supervisory meetings with students, in this single office, there were no problems at all. Sometimes I filled the office with peaceful music, which was not possible in a shared space. I now could secure a time to concentrate on my work without people coming and going. It felt like I could endure everything as long as I had my own small but single office. 'I am blessed,' I whispered.

Then five months later, I received an email from a senior member of staff. The message said that my office, in accordance with the University's restructuring of space, was now required by the University's Directorate. 'It is my understanding that there is still space for you in your previous shared office.' I paused and blinked my eyes twice. The senior colleague went on say that he himself had raised the matter with a member of the management team. A sympathetic note. The email ended with the following. 'Thank you for your understanding.' Unfortunately, it did not give me any comfort though. And the last sentence, 'Thank you for your understanding,' rather provoked me—I could not understand it at all, I could not accept it. I closed my eyes. An earthquake hit me deep inside. My safe haven, a single office, would now go. A place that helped me survive would be destroyed. 'Enough, enough.' I finally decided to resign.

Yes, *finally* . . . that means I had thought about resigning before. It is a long story. I arrived only one day before my first class—regarding a complicated visa system, the University's support system was not managed well. This had had a negative impact on my performance from the very beginning. I was squeezed to work in a shared office with three people—no privacy, no time to properly concentrate on work. I was to digest frequent institutional changes that staff were not consulted on—a lot of confusion and demoralisation. The list goes on and on. But again, I was still grateful for having a job, for being a professor. It was true. And there was no guarantee that my experience was unique to this particular university. For instance, the visa. Strictly speaking, my late arrival was not the University's fault. By making the visa system as complicated as possible, the country did not seem to welcome immigrants in theory. And in this age of neoliberalism, many universities are busy with budget-cuts and restructuring to uphold the ideology of competitiveness. Academics are squeezed to work and compete. It was not the life I expected. Stress began to eat away at me.

Then why no resignation earlier? It was my mother. She had a health issue, high blood pressure. She was diagnosed some years after my father had died. I was a teenager when I lost my father. What had cost his life? High blood pressure. I had enough reasons to be worried about. Since I had become a professor, which was great news, her health had got far better. She said that was because she was happy. My brother also said, 'Mother is now much healthier, thanks to you!' The human body sometimes works in a mysterious way. And the last thing I could do was to disturb the progress of mother's health—by breaking the news that I had resigned; that I was no longer a professor. I once asked myself though, 'This is my life. Why should I put my mother first?' Yes, it might sound harsh, but I did not have to think of my mother. It was my business. Then a quick thought hit me. 'My mother has put me first, almost always. She sacrificed immensely.' Indeed, beyond description. And I decided to keep going. It could never be compared to my mother's sacrifice, but I thought it was my turn. A little thing that I could do for my mother—to keep her happy, to keep her healthy. Some may say, 'That's pathetic.' But I decided to remain as a professor for my mother's sake.

And there was the single office as well—a safe haven, as I called it. Of course, my own office, which I desperately wanted but unexpectedly obtained, did not solve all the problems. But it did lessen my stress and did help me survive. Still, I could sense that something was going on inside me. I felt like I had become gradually cynical, just like many people here. When I started to work and observed my colleagues, sometimes friendly alarm bells rang. When I first arrived, I had to explain to others why I had come late. Understandably I mentioned a visa issue resulted from confusion within Human Resources. 'Welcome to A [this place]!' said one colleague who had a similar problem. As a newcomer, I had found it slightly difficult to understand. But as time went by, I could understand why. And I was not surprised when other people talked about their secret wishes to move to other universities. They even sent me a new job advertisement and encouraged me to apply. It was a very kind gesture, but a sad idea.

Soon I found myself being increasingly cynical—'Well, this is A!' 'I knew it. After all, this is A!' 'Whatever. Because . . . this is A!' This became quite problematic when, for example, I covered an Open Day event as a staff member. Knowing my true feeling about my own university, it was incredibly difficult for me to pretend that this university could be attractive and the best choice for prospective students. I realised it clearly when one applicant asked me a question. 'In your opinion, what's the best aspect of this university?' I moved my head towards the window, to avoid the questioner's eyes. 'Well, that's a wonderful question to ask, but a difficult one to answer.' Then I just offered a textbook answer, if I may say so.

But more importantly, from some point onwards, I began to pass my stress on to others. One day, when I had a phone conversation with Human Resources about confusing administrative measures, I suddenly saw myself raising my voice—it had never happened before. Probably the most devastating thing was that I slowly began to feel unhappy with . . . students. I never expressed this feeling openly. I never told anyone about it. I was still kind to my students. But deep inside, I knew it. And this broke my heart, deeply. I was angry with myself. I hated myself. All this emerged, even with my safe haven—the single office. But now that it was gone, I had no courage to continue. Of course I could just go on, like my colleagues. We are not saints. At the end of the day, there is no perfect life. We hurt; we hate; we get cynical. But still. Yes, but still . . . I did not want to continue. I tried; I did try hard. I went on, thinking of my mother, being grateful for my peaceful little office. Now, it was time to try in another way. I decided to mobilise my courage.

I was realistic enough to know that the decision would cost me several important things. First, my position. I would no longer be a professor now. If my mother knew this, there could be some consequences. Having worked as a professor already, however, I thought that was enough. Next, this would mean that I would be unemployed, at least for the time being. In other words, I had to face a financial problem. Fortunately, I have saved the most of my money while I was working. So a temporary solution there. All of this would mean, quite simply, uncertainty—a great deal of uncertainty. Without a formal position, without a stable income, I threw myself into a foggy world. A resignation based on one's conscience is not that romantic—it is a fight, fight against reality. It is such a violent conversation within oneself. You might need to ask yourself: Do you have enough energy to endure that fight? Are you prepared to take on that responsibility? Sometimes one may have that energy, sometimes not. On this occasion, at first, I did not know how to answer those questions. Mysteriously though, I realised that everything was meant to happen—maybe from the very beginning.

KAL 858 . . . I said to myself. The case that had defined my life since my early 20s; the case that had engineered my PhD; the case that had made me a professor. I used to regard this case as my destiny. At the twenty-fifth memorial ceremony in 2012, when I was invited to present my PhD thesis, I promised that I would not forget the case. I declared KAL 858 as my lifetime task. A lifetime task? This can be a bit of exaggeration, I thought. But I was serious. I felt that I owed the case something, I owed the families of the missing passengers a debt. As a scholar, I wanted to do something more—I wanted to keep working on the case. So I decided to do a new book project. But many people told me that I should move on. 'For your career, you should see the bigger picture. This one case study alone will not help you.' I was offended, at first. With several people saying the same thing, however, I began to think differently. Leaving aside that advice, to be honest, I myself seemed to be exhausted. I thus became hesitant to proceed with my plan. And becoming a professor meant there was not enough time for my own work—a lot of teaching and various administrative duties. I gradually forgot the case along with my new book project.

And now, the year 2017 was coming—the thirtieth anniversary of the case of KAL 858. If I resumed my project, I would be able to publish a book in 2017. Yes, it would be possible, if I would no longer be a professor—I could have enough time to write. I did not plan it, but this book, if published, would be something to commemorate the thirtieth anniversary. An unexpectedly meaningful project there . . . is that why I had struggled so far? I became more than ever convinced that it was time to resign. 'Professorship? I might be able to get another position later. But the thirtieth anniversary? Well, that would never come again . . . '

It seems that ghosts of KAL 858 have called me. I seemed to find my destiny again. As Laurent Binet (2013) said, when you take a special interest in a particular subject, everything appears to bring you back to it. I felt warm, as if my empty mind had become full of something. There is no guarantee that I could finish the book project though. But I would try, I would do my best. I could not identify it exactly, but it felt like some strange confidence was haunting me. Not so sure, but I could feel that something was there—something that waited for me, something that made me believe, and something that gave me strength. I was nodding my head. 'All this happened, because there was meaning.' I might be wrong, but decided to trust myself. So here is my final decision. A happy resignation.

* * *

20 July 2010, Tokyo Haneda Airport. A small plane, owned by the Japanese government, just landed at the airport. About twenty people were standing in front of the plane. They seemed to be waiting for a signal. Then three people in the front line suddenly opened their big umbrellas. Someone with a white suit and sunglasses rushed towards the umbrellas and got in a black car, which was right next to the plane. This black car, being guarded by several other black cars, headed off somewhere. Later a police car with red-blue lights joined them and led the motorcade. The black car in question was welcomed several times by groups of reporters and camera flashes along the way. Then the car arrived at the villa owned by former Japanese Prime Minister Yukio Hatoyama. Surely, something was happening . . .

Everything indicated that the person in the black car must have been a highly significant and politically sensitive figure—significant enough to use the Japanese government's aircraft and stay at the former prime minister's mansion; sensitive enough to warrant heavy security measures and attract a crowd of journalists and spotlights. Who was this person? It was someone who had once used a Japanese alias, Mayumi Hachiya. It was the same one who was believed to have bombed a plane killing 115 people. And it was the same one who had been sentenced to death as a terrorist . . . Yes, this person was Hyunhee Kim.

The following day, Kim was holding a knife. And a man was standing right beside her. There was nothing dangerous though—she was cooking for this man, Koichiro Iizuka, the son of Yayeko Taguchi. They had met each other in South Korea one year before. According to Kim, Koichiro's mother had taught her Japanese while she was trained as a spy in North Korea. Importantly, Kim confessed that Koichiro's mother had been abducted from Japan. Ever since this confession in 1987, the abduction problem became a thorny issue between Japan and North Korea. The Japanese government wanted to put more pressure on North Korea by inviting Kim to Japan. That was why the former terrorist, according to the official findings, was welcomed like a VIP or movie-star in Japan.

In the magnificent villa, Kim said to a reporter: 'I told Koichiro [when we met last year] that I would be his mother. And I promised him to make delicious food if we meet next time' (SBS 2010). She looked very relaxed and happy. The next day, Kim boarded a helicopter. The Japanese government offered her a luxury sightseeing tour. The terrorist became a tourist. 'Mount Fuji . . . It was too foggy to see it, unfortunately,' said Kim smiling with a hand gesture. The following day, Kim got into the same black car again and headed back to the airport. Just like her arrival a few days before, tight security measures and the police motorcade were arranged. She then returned to South Korea by the Japanese government's aircraft.

* * *

Part of my decision to resign was concerned with my conscience as a free-spirited scholar. I often thought about the meaning of *conscience*. Why do we have it? And how does it work? At some point, I came to realise that my military service might have something to do with this puzzle.

South Korea maintains a conscription system, so does North Korea, as the Korean peninsula is divided into two countries. The compulsory military service is just one example of the results of the tragic ongoing war. At first I thought that I did not have to do the service. That was because my father, a civil servant, was designated as a person of national merit after he had passed away. According to the law, a child of national honourees could be exempted from the mandatory military service. That was what I heard. But I still wanted to go to the military. 'Every man should do this service. I'd like to do my duty as a man.' Yes, I was a man.

There was and still is a popular saying in South Korea: 'One becomes human, when one goes to the military.' Simply it means that you would become a proper adult man, only after you finish the military service. Nowadays this logic is frequently challenged by various groups of people, notably feminists. But the glorification of military duty has been working as a powerful discourse for a very long time. As an ordinary young man, I myself was no exception. 'This is the national duty of every man. I should do it.' And just because I was the child of a national honouree, I did not want to ignore a *sacred duty*. 'It's an excuse . . . and I will do this duty in the toughest unit.' So I began planning to enlist in the Marine Corps. Probably I wanted to be an example: 'Look at him. He does his military service, even though he didn't have to do. What a great man!'

It eventually turned out that I did have to do the military service. The child of military national honourees, not the all honourees, could be exempted from the service. Well, to me, it did not make any difference because I was willing to go to the military anyway. After careful consideration I decided to enlist in the Army, not the Marine Corps. I finished my sacred duty. Then did I become a *proper adult*? Did I become a *real man*? Maybe and maybe not. Maybe . . . in the sense that I diligently learnt how to use a gun, how to obey orders and how to kill people. Maybe not . . . in the sense that I decided not to continue to learn those skills. Maybe . . . in the sense that I vividly witnessed people being beaten, North Korea was demonised and women were sexualised. Maybe not . . . in the sense that I decided not to continue to participate in these systems.

In the military, I learnt and witnessed something that I would not accept or practise happily. I was inspired by peace and feminist movements. And that was how I as a member of the Reserve Forces became a conscientious objector. In South Korea once men finish their national military service, they automatically belong to the Reserve Forces. It means that they have a duty, upon their discharge from the regular military, to attend an annual military training for some time. I had already attended several training sessions earlier, but my conscience did not allow me to just keep going like that. I had to do something. I did not want to make it big though—I wanted to proceed in a rather quiet manner; I did not plan to talk about it openly.

According to the law, I was then summoned to the police station. The message said that I needed to be questioned at the station and pay a fine. That was the first time in my life when I was subjected to police interrogation. I sat in front of a police officer in charge who then started writing a document on the computer. I quickly looked at it. The document said, 'The accused [. . .] a summary and absence trial . . . ' And I was supposed to pay a fine. It seemed like I had already admitted that I had done something wrong, although I did not have any chance to speak. I woke up suddenly.

'Excuse me sir . . . Could you allow me to tell you why I didn't attend the military training?' Still, I did not want to talk about my *real* reason. The police hesitated, and said. 'Well . . . if you want, yes . . . tell me.' Remember: do not make it public. 'I . . . refused to attend the training based on my conscience. I support other conscientious objectors as well.' Whoops. I was surprised by what I said. The police took off his glasses and stared at me with a tricky face. 'Oh, I see . . . then you can talk about this in front of a judge, if you want.' I did not need to make things complicated like that—I could just pay my fine at the station. 'Okay . . . then let me go to the court. When is it?' Whoops again. 'What? So you want a trial . . . are you sure?' asked the police in a surprised tone, as if this had not happened before. He hurriedly phoned someone and told me. 'Well . . . tomorrow morning at 9:00.' I went to the court and explained my reason for objecting to the military training. The result? I had to pay my fine, but a little surprise there. The judge decided to let me pay only half of my original fine.

The story did not end there. According to the law, I still had to attend the military training even after I had paid my fine. I would be punished again and again, until I attended the annual training that year. In order not to make things much worse, I went to the training in the end. For the same reason, in the following year, I did my duty as a reservist. Then again, my conscience began to call me. I could not just ignore it. So I refused to attend the training the next year—it was my last annual training as a reservist. I was summoned to the police station again. I expected that the procedure would be quite similar to the earlier case. I was mistaken . . . big time.

A police officer questioned me. 'Why didn't you go to the military training?' I talked about the things I had already explained two years ago. 'So, because of your conscience . . . well, that's fine, okay,' said the police and asked. 'Then tell me. Why did you go to the military in the first place?' 'That's because . . . ' The police interrupted me. 'Look. You already served in the Army, didn't you? But now you are talking about your conscience. How can a conscience change like that?' ' . . . ' I did not know how to answer. I

knew I got cold feet at that moment. The police said that I did not get a serious punishment before, as it was my first breach of duty. From the second
breach onwards, it would be different. Yes, indeed. As before, I went to the
court. But this time, I got fined ten times more. As before, I still had to attend
the training. But this time, I faced a serious consequence. Following one's
conscience could come at a cost.

But there is one thing that I feel grateful for—the military experience. I
became deeply interested in the Korean conflict and inter-Korean relations.
This experience led me to study the relevant subjects wishing to become a
scholar. Crucially it would encourage me to participate in the unification thesis competition and eventually would lead me to encounter the case of KAL
858. Then how did all this begin?

'Pain . . . ' I would say. There was an incident where I had to witness
an unintended consequence of the ongoing war. My close colleague was
expelled to a different unit because of a cruel act. This colleague physically
and mentally abused a subordinate soldier. To me, the colleague was just a
good and kind friend. But it seemed that the violent and hierarchical nature of
the military changed my colleague. Indeed, various types of violence including psychological violence had been and still are widespread in the military.
Before this colleague left, all the platoon members were called to gather in a
squad room. Everyone lined up on the long upper floor of the room, except
the soon-to-be-expelled who was standing alone below that floor. I looked
downwards to see my colleague. That was when I realised something: 'The
Korean peninsula is divided into the North and South. It is heartbroken. And
that's why we are here in the military. But even among us . . . we hurt each
other. How sad. Something is terribly wrong . . . '

Yes, it was sad enough that both Korean peoples were suffering from
the division. But even sadder because people internalised this division and
directed their anger towards their own kind. Not to mention the one who
was a target, the victim. The most disturbing thing in this? I later would find
myself verbally abusing my subordinate . . . it was so painful for me to realise
what I had done.

*   *   *

*19 December 2011, Pyongyang. Kim Jong-il, 'general secretary of the Workers
Party of Korea, chairman of the DPRK National Defense Commission and
supreme commander of the Korean People's Army,' died (KCNA 2011).
According to the Korean Central News Agency, a state-run media organisation, he 'passed away of a serious illness at 08:30 on 17 December.' It was
said that North Korean people were engulfed in indescribable sadness for
this sudden loss.*

The Sankei Shimbun, a right-wing newspaper in Japan, was quick to contact Hyunhee Kim. In her interview she said, 'I knew he would die at some point, but I was surprised that his death came so early. I regret that he, as the one who had ordered me to bomb a South Korean plane, didn't admit his responsibility or apologise for it' (Cho 2011). Kim also talked about the abduction issue, which led the Japanese government to invite her to visit Japan the year before. 'I have said that it would be difficult to solve the abduction problem as long as he was alive. Now that he has gone, it will become easier to work out the problem.'

* * *

One of my childhood dreams was to become a school teacher. But my high school teacher once said to me. 'No, I hope you will become a university professor.' I wondered what my teacher would make of my resignation.

When it came to teaching, I took students' motivation very seriously. Hence in every first session of new classes, I always had a brief round of self-introduction and a quick survey. I first let students fill out a short questionnaire: why they chose to study their subject field, what they expect from my course and what their dreams are. Then I invited students to introduce themselves based on the questionnaire. Importantly I talked about myself, including my dream, first, before students started. That way I believed that some kind of connection could be formed, a small step towards getting to know each other. According to my observation, most students seemed to like this short session. I was convinced that this interactive experience at the start of the course would play an important role throughout the whole semester. Another key point of this activity was that I reminded students of their motivations and dreams when I gave them feedback for their final assessment. With students' replies and thank-you notes, it became clear that they appreciated this reflective self-introduction opportunity.

Nonetheless, it was not so straightforward. When another new semester started, I had a self-introduction session as usual. At first, everything seemed alright. When about half of students finished their talks, I noticed that one student looked somewhat annoyed. She stared at me and said something to her classmate next to her. Maybe she does not like this session, I thought. Others kept talking about themselves one by one. But now she put her head down on the desk. I became slightly alarmed. 'Maybe she thinks it's boring . . . ' Then suddenly she stood up, with an unhappy face, and walked towards an entrance. 'Bang!' She slammed the door and left. I was surprised and somewhat embarrassed as a teacher, but just continued. At the same time, I realised that I might have forced students to talk about themselves. I might have suggested that students should have dreams. It was possible that some people felt pressured. After a few minutes, she returned. On her way back to the seat, she grumbled. I quickly wrapped up the session.

From then I became slightly intimated in that class. She almost always came to the session, and almost always looked a bit aggressive. During my lecture, she sometimes cynically laughed at me. I tried to avoid her whenever possible. When I spoke in front of students, I looked at the right side of the classroom; she was always on the left side of the room. I usually held a group discussion at the end of each session. When I had to ask her group questions, I did not make eye contact with her. At some point, I said to myself, 'What am I doing? Why should I be afraid of a student?' I struggled. Now, with the middle of the semester an assessment period came. It was a presentation. Naturally and understandably, I was worried about hers. At the same time, I was very curious about the presentation. When it was her turn, things appeared to run smoothly. Not bad, I thought. When she finished her presentation and passed by me, I could hear something. 'Shit, he doesn't like my presentation.' I could not believe that she used the S-word. I felt insulted. But I pretended not to hear the S-word. 'Have I done something wrong?' I wondered. 'Should I say something?' I kept wondering. Then I stood up, and looked at students. 'Okay . . . next please.'

You may wonder how my actual teaching went. The very first session in the UK, something like this: 'Right . . . welcome everyone. Thank you for coming. This is our very first session and there are several things to go through. Uhmm, first, my name is Sungju Park-Kang, but please call me Sungju. If you call me, for example, Professor Sungju Park-Kang, you will be . . . kicked out of the class!' Students giggled. 'Okay? So . . . just call me Sungju.' I smiled. 'Then let me ask you a quick question please. When did you arrive? I mean, for this semester.' Some students answered: one month before, one week before, three days before. 'Great. Well, as for me, just yesterday,' I paused. 'I don't want to go into detail, but I only arrived one day before this first session. Unfortunately, this means I didn't have much time to prepare, so you might be disappointed throughout this course. And I'd like to apologise in advance, if that would be the case.' No particular reactions from students. 'But! I can tell you this: I will try to do my best . . . okay?' I said with a hand gesture. 'And . . . all you have to decide is what to do with the time that is given to you.' I paused, and asked students. 'Anyone familiar with these words?' I walked through the classroom. 'Anyone?' No replies.

'Gandalf! *The Lord of the Rings*?' I kindly showed the picture of Gandalf on my slides. Students laughed. 'Yes. The thing is, I only arrived yesterday, but as Gandalf said, I will do my best with the time that is given to me . . . okay?' Students smiled. 'Right. Then let's move on to our syllabus. And the copies are here . . . So, has everyone got the syllabus?' Students nodded their heads. 'Good. Well, given my circumstances, I mean I only arrived yesterday, so this syllabus is not completed yet. But you can see some basic information there, so let's look at them together.' I explained a course schedule, reading list and so on.

When it came to assessment, I said this. 'I am not going to evaluate your intellectual capabilities. Okay? Rather, I would say: if you do your best, I can see that in your presentation. If you do your best, I can read that in your essay.' I walked through the room again. 'This may sound quite boring, but your sweat will not betray you. If you do your best, you will get something you deserve. Well, maybe not always. But even then, it will get back to you later in one way or another. I can tell you this from my own experience. Your sweat, will not, betray you . . . ' I said it stressing each two-word. 'Okay? Right, more specific information will be provided later. But at this stage, just remember this: Do your best. Your sweat will not betray you.'

The second session. 'Okay. Welcome back everyone. Thank you for coming. Today, I'd like to start with this image.' My slide showed a university institute's logo, which read in English 'Center for Korean Studies' and in Korean 'Hangukhak yeonguso.' 'Can anyone tell us what you see here?' No replies. 'Can anyone read this Korean word? Or if you can't read, then what about in English?' One student answered, 'Center for Korean Studies?' 'Yes!! Thank you!' The student only read what was written. It was easy. But I rather intentionally praised the student in a loud voice, to encourage others to participate also. 'Then, what's the difference between Korean Studies and . . . Hangukhak?' 'Their pronunciations are different,' the same student answered. 'Yes, of course! Thank you. But if I may go further, there is more than that. Korean Studies and Hangukhak . . . Can anyone guess what it is?' No replies. Then, 'I think Hangukhak is a translation of Korean Studies . . . ?' 'Yes, great. Thank you! We are almost there, yes. So Hangukhak is a Korean translation of the English term Korean Studies. Now, I wonder if anyone can go a bit further?' I walked through the classroom. Silence went on.

'Okay, then let me give you a clue. In Korean, Hanguk means South Korea and hak means studies. Hanguk is South Korea and hak is studies . . . can anyone go further now?' I moved my hands up and down, encouraging students to answer. 'Hangukhak is South Korean Studies?' 'Yes!! Finally. Thank you. That's it. So, here again. Hangukhak should be translated into South Korean Studies, but in this image, that's not the case. It is just Korean Studies. Why? Because in the academic community Hanguk represents both Koreas, not South Korea. South Korea represents Korea as the universal.'

I changed a slide. 'So, as you can see the title "Food for thought," I would say the translation issue we have just discussed is telling us about how knowledge is constructed. It's a sort of jargon, but this is called positionality. Things become different depending on where you stand. In North Korea, Korean

Studies is called Chosunhak . . . In South Korea, it is Hangukhak. And as you have seen, in the academic community, Korean Studies is usually translated into Hangukhak. So there is this contestedness there, if you like. Power relations within knowledge.' I paused before continuing. 'I'm not saying that we should call Korean Studies Chosunhak, or Hangukhak. The point is . . . we need to be sensitive about this contested nature of knowledge. Try to be careful, always. Okay?' Several students nodded.

'By the way, food for thought.' I pointed to the title of the slide, then to bananas on the front desk. I brought bananas for students. 'So food is here, if you are hungry.' Students smiled. 'Right! Then before we move on, one more thing please. Uhmm, some of you may not like this idea, but if I may, I will not upload my slides to our course website.' I paused.

'Why? Going back to the discussion of positionality, these slides are based on my own reading of our materials. So, my own positionality there. Of course, I tried to be as *objective* as possible. But given the very contested nature of knowledge, the slides might have been filtered through my own perspectives, in one way or another. That's why I will not upload these slides. You should not be confined into the text on my slides. You need to read the materials by yourself. Otherwise, my interpretation would overshadow your understanding. You must read by yourself first, and need to come up with your own idea. Okay?'

Only a few students nodded their heads. 'Of course, some of you may want to have the slides. In that case, please let me know. Then I will send you the slides by email. But otherwise, in principle, I will not upload them. Does it make sense?' More students nodded. 'Great! Thank you for your understanding. Then, let's move on.'

The third session. 'Again, welcome everyone. Thank you for coming.' I walked through the classroom. 'Today, I'd like to start by telling you something that other teachers would never say.' I came back to the front and looked at students. 'Please, do not trust me.' I paused. Someone giggled. 'Please do not believe what I say . . . ' Students stared at me. 'Let me put it into context. Do you remember what we discussed at the beginning of the last class?' 'Bananas!' Everyone laughed. 'Yes, bananas! Thank you. That is, our food-for-thought discussion on positionality, right? The contested nature of knowledge production.' I came to the middle of the room.

'Apart from my slides that I mentioned last week, everything I say in this classroom is open to interpretation. You must not take it as it is. Everything is contested in one way or another. Nothing is fixed. So when I say "Do not trust me," it is not about me—Sungju as a person. But rather it is about the politics of contestedness, positionality. You need to form your own agenda. You need to form your own interpretation. If you wish, you can take my talk as a sort of stepping stone to move around. But other than that, please do not accept what

I say as it is. Does it make sense?' Some nodded their heads. 'Okay. Then like last week, first, food for thought. And importantly, there are bananas again!'

Yes, I enjoyed teaching. But I sometimes became a bit frustrated about the bureaucratic nature of teaching environment. My work email received a lot of messages from the University. One such example was a student attendance monitoring report on a weekly basis. 'The following students have been identified as not attending scheduled events as specified within the Student Attendance Monitoring policy.' Every student had their own ID card and needed to register their attendance whenever they had a class by tagging an electronic monitoring system. If they did not tag, it was assumed that they were absent. All this information was collected and each student's absence rate was calculated. Then this result was sent to each personal tutor of students. That way all students' attendance could be monitored automatically. How convenient. I, however, felt that I was *forced* to monitor, or more harshly speaking *spy* on my students. As someone who has conducted a long-term research on KAL 858, I was familiar with the issue of surveillance or the like. Of course, in strict terms, it was not surveillance. But in practice, I had a similar feeling.

It is definitely necessary to check students' attendance. This could be done manually during the class, by checking an attendance sheet. That was all. I had another thing in mind. I would have called students' names one by one. With calling each student, I would make eye contact every time—connecting with students to some extent. Well, to be fair, if there was a huge class this could be problematic—let's say a class of more than one hundred students. But that is an exceptional case. Even in this case, students for example could be invited to mark their own name on the sheet. But with the electronic system, that sort of traditional method should have been thrown away. Yes, in some ways, the new system was convenient as it was done automatically. A lot of loopholes though. When I happened to pass by one lecture room, I witnessed several students tagging their cards in front of the door and running away. Their absence could not be detected through the system. And electronic cards sometimes did not work properly. The cards were just out of order, which meant absence was recorded falsely. Or sometimes students just forgot to bring their cards. Again, it was assumed they were absent.

As a personal tutor, I was responsible for caring for more than thirty students. And students, due to the card issue, very often asked me to correct or record their attendance manually. More than that. Based on this report, if the absence rate reached a certain level, students were given a warning. And teachers were asked to have a meeting personally with the student in question and report back to the relevant administration body. The thing is that in many cases, before this warning was issued, students already contacted the administration to explain why their absence record was incorrect. But somehow, the record remained the same on the system. And they got a higher level of warning next time. That was why, apart from the surveillance issue, I did not trust the automatic system. It was also not convenient to receive such a monitoring report every week. Other teachers might say differently. But for me, it was obvious: bureaucratically convenient, but humanely unhelpful.

I had similar feelings, but in a different context, when I first arrived here. As a lecturer, one of my top priorities before the semester started was to complete syllabi. I surely had a general idea on how to do it. But I realised that it was far more complicated. First of all, it was very long—usually twenty pages or so. The rationale behind this seemed to be that almost all the information students needed, including standardised administrative instructions, should have been provided there. Yes, I agreed. But when a syllabus was about twenty pages, it became a different matter. Far too detailed bureaucratic instructions there. Most of all, however, making syllabi seemed very mechanical. The basic description and contents of a course, including evaluation methods and weights, should have not changed. Even a reading list should have remained the same. In principle, they could be revised. In practice, there was not enough time and it was highly discouraged. That was because it demanded a lot of paperwork and a long approval procedure to go through.

Apparently, the only part I could change was a weekly schedule. There was almost no room for teachers' autonomy. To be fair, there were some advantages. It secured continuity and stability to sustain and run the course. And teachers did not have to think much about the syllabus each time. They could just follow the given instructions. It was easy to make a syllabus—mostly cut and paste, and cut and paste. The key point, however, was that each teacher did not matter, because they could be replaced by someone else when the management wished. Indeed, many of my colleagues were fixed-term employed for one or two years. It appeared that the current syllabus format did not value individual teachers' creativity, flexibility and research interests. Teachers were like replaceable tools on a regular basis. They were almost like batteries—quickly changeable and easily disposable. What mattered here were productivity, uniformity and bureaucratic directives.

Leaving aside the above, for my teaching sessions, I would do everything I could. Most of all, I had a teaching diary. My preparation would start from there: I would do brainstorming about the upcoming session. Then I would work on a draft of the slides I would use in the session. I would revise and revise again. When I was satisfied, I would print them out. On that copy, I would make a script as well. Not word by word, but some main points. Importantly, some jokes also, to make sure I remembered them. And I would prepare several handouts to distribute to students. Sometimes, there was extra but significant information to digest. Giving the relevant handouts would help students keep them in mind. And I would hasten to add the following message: 'Please read them and utilise them. Otherwise, we would just waste our trees and environment. That's too bad! Please don't make me feel guilty, if you know what I mean.'

Next, I would buy bananas. Yes, bananas, fruits. Although it was not my fault, my late arrival caused troubles for me to properly prepare for the semester. My potentially poorly managed performance would embarrass me. At the end of the day, however, eventually the *victims* would be my students. Related to this preemptive guilt, I wanted to do something good for students. That was partly how the idea of food came up. I would try to select the best-looking bananas at a store. This selection process would be quite picky. If these bananas were for myself, I would not mind that much.

Once the selection was finished with a satisfactory result, I would go to my classroom in advance. First I would put my bananas in a hidden space around the teacher's desk, along with the handout materials, if any. It was important for me to choose the timing. There should be no one there, because I would do some rehearsal. Yes, indeed. I would stand alone in front, and looked around the room imagining there were students. And say, 'Welcome everyone! Thank you for coming.' No, maybe a slightly different one. 'Thank you for coming. Welcome!' Uhmm, what about this? 'Good afternoon. Welcome! Thank you for coming.' Sometimes I would practice my gesture. I would walk through the room looking at the left and right, as if students were sitting there. Yes, seriously.

Once this rehearsal went well, I would come back to my office, take some rest. Then, I would look into my slides and script again, to detect something to add or correct. Until the last moment before the class, I would keep doing it and practising. But one more thing there. Around fifteen to twenty minutes before anyone arrived in the classroom, I would assure that my slides were already on the screen. And I would take out my best selected bananas, along with the handouts, from the hidden space and put them in one of the desks on the first row. That way, when students entered the room they would feel, 'Hmmm, things are ready here.'

Once the class started, I would deliver the session as best as I could. By now I had practised enough to memorise most of my slides, so I would be able to just talk through without looking at the screen. Before I suggested having a short break, I would ask students, 'Do you have any questions?' I would accommodate questions or comments if any. Otherwise, I would say, 'If not, bananas for ten minutes please!' Then I would go to a toilet, then go out to take a walk. I would think about how to proceed with the rest of the session. Or I would just stay in a toilet, one of the empty rooms there—to look into the slides and script.

At the second half of the session, I again would do my best. Once the talk ended, I would invite students for a discussion session. I would divide them into small groups. After each group had its own discussion, I would open a whole class discussion. I would encourage students to exchange each group's idea or ask me a question. There could be some questions or comments that I would not be sure how to deal with. In that case, I would look into those issues and get back to students in the next session. When the session was finished and students had gone, I would remain in the empty room for a while; I would close my eyes and do some reflection. This is where my teaching diary came again. I would write down how the session went. If well, why? If not, why not? So, from a teaching diary, bananas, rehearsal, to a teaching diary again. That was how I did my teaching.

The last teaching week before the Christmas break. I was preparing for my session. As usual, I had already bought bananas. This time, I had something more: small cakes. Yes, it was Christmas. Everything was in order, and I was finalising the slides. 'Knock, knock.' I heard something. Someone was standing outside my office. I slowly opened the door. 'Oh, hello!' There were two students from my class. 'Sorry, we don't want to disturb you, but just wanted to give you this.' There was something wrapped up in a red-white paper, symbolising Christmas. 'And also this . . . ' A handmade card. What a nice surprise! Totally unexpected. I became almost paralysed. 'Wow . . . I don't know what to say. Thank you so much. I . . . really appreciate it. Wow, I'm really surprised. Thank you!!' I did not open the present or card. In Korea people would not usually do that. Opening the gift in front of the giver is not a Korean custom. Instead, I closed the door. I did not know what to do. Wow, amazing. I put the wrapped-up gift on the desk. I gently pushed it with my finger. It felt soft. Hmmm, what would it be? I was so thrilled that I could hear my heart beating. Now I cautiously, very carefully removed the wrap, leaving it almost undamaged.

There, I could see a Christmas tree. Not a real one, but an image of the tree on a jumper. On its dark blue background, snow was falling. At the bottom, various colourfully wrapped presents. And there was something on a big yellow Christmas tree-topper. A little button with a music symbol. Out of curiosity, I pressed it. 'Lallala Lallala Lallalalala . . . ' It was a Christmas carol! Full of joy, I opened the card as well. There were some cute drawings, which must have been done by students themselves. Importantly, I could see students' names written in Korean. And also this note, 'Komapsumnida' meaning thank you in Korean. A pure, genuine surprise—I was overwhelmingly touched and honoured so I kissed the jumper and the card. A few hours later, the time has come. In front of the classroom, I was a little shyly standing—I was wearing that Christmas jumper. Students smiled. Several of them even took my picture with phones. That day, the session started with a Christmas carol.

I loved teaching. At first, teaching as a job sounded quite burdensome. 'Do I know enough to lecture anyone?' I asked myself. 'Am I good enough to be an example for students?' I wondered. 'What if students don't like me?' Well, I was sensitive. 'What about my English?' Yes, it was not my first language. And what did I do? Preparation and practice. I was pleased when students laughed during the class. I felt valued when students took notes for my talk. I felt thrilled when I learnt something in the course of preparation. In a word, I did not regard myself as a teacher, a professor—I just wanted to be someone who *shares* something. I did not think I was teaching; I thought I myself was learning. This idea, teaching as sharing and learning, made me feel a lot better.

And I tried to be as creative as possible. When I talked about old Korean history, I wanted to teach in a different way. So I brought something to the classroom: Korean coins and banknotes that had important historical figures and symbols on their surface. I circulated them among students and could see them becoming much more engaged. I even sang a song at some point. That was when I had a session about the Japanese occupation. A famous traditional Korean song called *Arirang*. I was not a great singer in any way at all, but students applauded when I sang. All this made me begin to think that I might have something for teaching.

But the tricky thing is, I hated grading. Please do not get me wrong. It was totally okay for me to read students' assignments. I enjoyed it. I could learn a lot from their writing. I could get to know them from their presentations. Giving comments was okay as well. This was my opportunity to show students that I cared about them. I could tell them how not to repeat the mistakes I myself made before. And I was delighted when students said, 'Thank you for your detailed comments!' Indeed, delivering comments and hearing back from students made me more motivated.

When it came to numerical evaluations, however, I very much struggled. That was because in one way or another I had to *judge* students. It felt like I forced students to line up. 'Everyone, stand in line! And you, you and you. Move forwards. And you, you and you, move backwards.' Numbering students is a judgmental and hierarchical process. For me, it was such an uncomfortable task. When I was a PhD student and worked as a teaching assistant, I had to do my first grading. I even thought, I hate grading so much that I could not become a professor. I wished I could do assessment without numbering; just giving comments would be good. Engaging is wonderful, but judging is not.

All in all, my empathetic approach seemed to pay off. I would receive positive messages from several students at the end of my first semester. Sometime later, my Head of School forwarded me the following message from a student, who nominated me for the teaching award. 'This staff member is different from many lecturers in that he encourages more discussion than just giving a lecture based on his notes, he encourages self-study and not just to take his word for it, He cares about his students and makes the classroom a friendly forum of discussion. He brings us bananas too! He's great.' I was truly honoured, and humbled.

However, not all students would have the same thought. In my second semester, I got complaints. Most of all, it said that I did not upload my slides to the course website, because I did not care about my students. *Did not care about* . . . I was deeply saddened. I had already explained during the class why I would not upload the slides. But it did not matter. What mattered was what students felt. If students say I do not care about them, it is my fault. It was like I was . . . impeached. I could not face students anymore. They would not listen to me whatever I say—they did not have confidence in me. I lost courage. But to try to reach them, I decided to hold a session on the complaints as a whole. I tried to explain the things as much as I could. I wanted to resolve misunderstandings. To my surprise, I would get emails from several students later. They said that not everyone felt the same way; they thanked me for the bananas, a symbol of my care meaning I gave them a lot of care. It was the students who broke my heart, but it was also the students who kept me warm.

* * *

18 June 2012, Seoul. TV Chosun, a South Korean media, aired its controversial programme. When I first heard the news that Hyunhee Kim was scheduled to appear on this television programme, it did not feel good. The families of KAL 858 had long wanted to meet and talk to Kim. Of course they did not know her address, as she was protected by the police and intelligence agency; so they put forward their demand in various other ways—through press conferences and demonstrations in front of the intelligence agency. They however could not hear anything from Kim or the related parties. But Kim was going to be on the television. How would the families feel about this?

At the same time, I wondered: 'why this programme?' The television show in question was produced by a cable news network of The Chosun Ilbo—*the largest newspaper in South Korea, a leading conservative media outlet. It consistently attacked the reinvestigation campaign for KAL 858, labelling it a pro-North Korean or extreme left-wing movement. That is,* The Chosun Ilbo *was and still is the staunch defender of the official findings of the case. Indeed, it was the very first media organisation in the world that conducted an interview with Kim in 1989. This exclusive interview was arranged with the help of the intelligence agency and published in* The Monthly Chosun, *a magazine owned by the same newspaper. So it was not difficult to expect that what Kim was going to say on the programme would hurt the families of KAL 858.*

'The Current Affairs Talk Show Pan, *today's guest is the bomber of KAL, Ms Hyunhee Kim. Welcome!' said a man presenter and stood up (TV Chosun 2012). A woman presenter stood up as well. With a sound effect being played as in entertainment talk shows, Kim walked into the studio. The two present- ers bowed to Kim and they shook hands together. This was her first appear- ance on Korean television in fifteen years since she got married in 1997. 'To begin with, as this is my first opportunity to appear on a domestic broadcast [in many years], to those who passed away and their families because of the bombing of KAL, I'd like to take this opportunity to deeply apologise again and seek their forgiveness,' said Kim in a quiet tone of her voice and looked downwards.*

The programme, consisting of two parts, went on for about one hour. 'Well, now after you were pardoned, in future . . . what would be the role given to you?' asked the man presenter. 'The Republic of Korea spared my life like this . . . because, North Korea still doesn't admit it. [. . .] So to me, keeping the truth of the case of KAL is the mission that I should do, I think,' nodded Kim. She also talked about the moment when she heard the news about the special pardon. 'At that moment, well, my feeling was, is it okay to be alive like this? At that time while I was studying about God, I was grateful to be allowed to live like this . . . what should I do to pay back? And my parents came to mind as well,' Kim finished, smiling very briefly and looked downwards, swal- lowing rather gently. The programme ended. The presenters bowed to Kim politely. She bowed to them.

I did not know what to say. From the very beginning of the programme, I became a little bit upset. That music, a melody . . . it was like an entertain- ment show. According to the official findings, she is a terrorist; and a lot of people were killed by this bomber. But now she has become a pop star. The music, it was not Kim's fault. But that was still too much. It made me just speechless. Apart from that, I had many questions about what Kim said. Take for example the North Korean leader's direct order that led Kim to bomb the plane. This is an incredibly important part. But the point is, there is no tan- gible evidence. This information is based on Kim's words only—no physical evidence to prove it. Of course, Kim's statement could be true, but I am not alone in posing this question. Even a foreign official had a similar thought. I obtained the Australian government's secret documents through a FOIA request. There was a memo left by an Australian official at the Department of Foreign Affairs and Trade: 'a key point, but is there evidence?' (DFAT 1988: 166).

Kim's passport was another tricky matter. According to a secret document of the South Korean Ministry of Foreign Affairs that I reviewed through the FOIA request, the passport was so poorly forged that a Japanese official could immediately detect it—that was why she was arrested. However, a starkly different evaluation was presented at the U.S. congressional hearing in February 1988. Clayton McManaway, Ambassador at Large for Counter-Terrorism at the Department of State: 'U.S. experts have concluded that the forged passports are of such high quality that they were almost certainly prepared by a government intelligence service. No terrorist group is known to have the capability to produce forgeries of this quality' (U.S. GPO 1989: 13).

What about the whole process of Kim's confession? For instance, according to the official findings Kim's first confessionary words were 'Sister, I am sorry.' Here, sister referred to the then woman investigator who was watching Kim at the time of her confession. What a drama . . . But the real drama was this: the intelligence agency admitted in 2004 that those words were made up as part of the government's propaganda strategy. Yes, it was a lie. Importantly, it indicated that various other statements could have been manipulated by the spy agency. Indeed, her confession about the explosives was not true either. The spy agency announced that the bombs planted on KAL 858 were C4 350 g and PLX 700 cc. They suggested that Kim had confessed all this. But it was later revealed that she had never said such things—the agency made up all these names and amounts. But Kim did not mention this sort of manipulation on the programme—not at all. So how could we possibly believe what she said on the television? How could we be sure that Kim was telling the truth?

Most importantly, I could not take Kim's apology: 'I'd like to take this opportunity to deeply apologise again and seek their forgiveness.' If she had really been sorry, she should not have appeared on the television in the first place. If she had really sought forgiveness, she should have mentioned all those manipulations on the television. As far as I know, the families of KAL 858 could not understand why Kim was granted a pardon; she had not spent even one day in a prison, not even one second. If she were a real terrorist, this should not have been allowed. But Kim was treated like a heroine—a special guest from North Korea protected by the South Korean authorities. Let's say she needed to be protected because she was the only key witness. Indeed, that was the government's position. If that is the case, she should testify in front of people whenever necessary. But where was she when the reinvestigation was under way? Why did she refuse to get interviewed when the truth was desperately needed? South Korea spared her life to let her testify as the witness? That does not make sense . . . She even married and had kids, while the families of KAL lost their spouses and children. I wonder if this is fair.

* * *

The things leading up to my resignation somehow brought me back to the days when I was writing a PhD thesis—the times full of twists and turns.

At some point in winter, unexplainable circumstances hit me hard. My PhD project on the case of KAL 858, which no one had ever tried, faced a huge crisis. My world was shaking. My head became empty. I went out for a walk. I wandered around the street. Suddenly I found myself in a church. I did not have any religion. And I did not know why I was there. I walked around the church. It was quiet. There were candles. I looked at them for a while. I felt that they were like me—they were shaking as well. I put forward both hands, surrounding the candles. It was warm. Then I stepped back. I placed my hands together, and bowed my head. I did not know why; it just naturally came. Then I went to the basement level. A little light, but not dark at all. Slightly chilly, but not cold at all. And various memorials there. I circled the whole basement. Then I stopped in front of a small window. Fragmented sunlight was coming through it, from the earth. Below the window, a small candle and a long chair. I sat down. 'Huhhh . . . ' And I looked at the window. 'I am tired. Can I continue my work?' I closed my eyes. Yes, I was tired, exhausted. That was because of . . . KAL 858.

I looked back on the first moment I encountered the case. It was when I had attended a national thesis competition organised by the government. Then I joined the reinvestigation campaigns. I worked with the families of the missing passengers. Against every odd, I wrote an MA thesis about this case, which became the first full academic work on the case ever. I later published a book based on the thesis. Upon my graduation, the TRC or a truth commission was launched. People suggested that I should apply for a position so that I would be able to reinvestigate the case of KAL. I did, but failed several times. It later turned out that the failure was partly due to my political commitments and writings. But I did not give up. I decided to do a PhD on this case, becoming an independent investigator. And here I was. After a long research journey, in the basement of a church.

I opened my eyes. I looked at the candle, then the window again. 'I did my best.' Yes, I did. 'I lived my life sincerely.' Yes, indeed. The only thing I would regret was, not finishing my PhD. But at least, part of my PhD work had already been published, which became the first academically charged publication on the subject in English. This led me to believe that I have done my *duty*. Well, it would be better if the PhD could be finished. But at that time, I thought I had done enough, I had fulfilled my mission.

Now, I wanted to get some rest. Probably *not* some, *but* the most fundamental rest of all. What was I thinking about? Yes, saying goodbye to the world. Strangely, I was not afraid at all. I was calm. I was ready, ready to go. I closed my eyes again. 'Yeah, that's it,' I nodded. Then a mysterious idea came up. 'If I die, I might be able to see Kim Jong-il.' It was the North Korean leader who, according to Hyunhee Kim the bomber, ordered the destruction of KAL 858. He had died just a year before. 'I would also be able to see Hyunhee Kim's partner agent.' He had committed a suicide when he was arrested with Kim. 'And . . . I could meet the missing passengers as well.' They were believed to be dead. Wait, what was I doing? I was making a list of interviewees . . .

It was that very moment when I heard something, a sort of music. 'La la-la, la-la la-lala-/ La la-la, la-la lala-la-/ La-la la-la, la-la-/ La . . . ' I opened my eyes. It was an organ melody, coming from the church's astronomical clock. Very soft, graciously peaceful—*In dulci jubilo*. Then, a warm liquid dropped from my eyes . . . and it reached my heart. 'Let's die, while writing. Let's go till the end.' Yes, the organ music saved me. The clock showed me the new light. By the way, I did know that the clock played the melody at noon. I had entered the church in the afternoon so I never expected to hear the music. But the clock also played at 3 p.m., which I was not aware of . . .

That night, I had a strange dream. Hyunhee Kim appeared in my dream. She walked towards me holding hands with another person. Probably on her right side, it looked like a man. I could not see the face of this man. Considering that they were holding hands together, there should be something between the two. I became convinced that the person next to Kim might have played an important role in the case of KAL 858—from the very beginning and, probably, even now. I obviously wanted to see the face. They came a step closer, then another step, and another one. Although I clearly identified Kim, I still could not see the face of the person next to her. I reached out my hand to them, and shouted with all my force: 'Hyunhee Kim! Hyunhee Kim! Hyunhee Kim!'

Then I woke up. I was not sure if I had shouted only in the dream or I actually had. What was clear was that I was sweating. This had rarely happened to me in my entire life. The dream felt like so real that I could not do anything once I woke up. It was still dark outside. I went to bed before 9 p.m. Yes, it was a bit early. But at some point, I had started going to sleep relatively early. I was not sure, but maybe since I had had a nervous breakdown as a university student in the course of the unification thesis scandal—the horrific nightmare and distress that I had in the evening in 2002 that changed my life. Indeed, without that experience, I most likely would not have to have such a strange dream. I was just sitting on the bed. For me, this dream seemed to reconfirm that the case of KAL 858 was my destiny. Facing an unexpected and enormous crisis, I decided to fully embrace my destiny.

From that day, all of my twenty-four hours were organised for almost only one purpose: the thesis. I had long been an early riser, but got up much earlier now—around at 3 a.m., sometimes at 2 a.m. After a brief wash, I headed to my office. While walking, I thought about what to write. It took about ten to fifteen minutes. Once I arrived, I went to a toilet. There, I prayed. Again, I had no religion but prayed. I looked at the mirror and whispered. 'Everything will be fine. Yes, that's right.' Then I closed my eyes, out of desperation. When

I opened the eyes, I looked at the mirror again—remembering what Paulo Coelho (2003: 171) said in *The Alchemist*: 'when you want something, all the universe conspires in helping you to achieve it.' Then I imagined the moment when I would finish my thesis. How wonderful. What a miracle. With that hope, with my smile, the ritual ended. This is how I prayed.

Then how did I write? In principle, I focused on only one thing—one section, one theme or one chapter. After praying, I turned on my computer and started to write straight away. Once I finished an initial part of the writing, I had breakfast in the common kitchen. It would be around at 5 or 6 a.m. My breakfast ended with an apple. Importantly, when I had this dessert I turned off the light. In a dark and quiet kitchen, while eating, I looked out of the window. Another fruit there—orange streetlights. All this made me feel peaceful, and purposeful.

With this renewed energy, I went out for a walk briefly, again thinking about what to write. Then I went on writing again. By 10 or 11 still in the morning, I would reach my goal. Yes, I have done for the day. With satisfaction, I enjoyed lunch. Then I went to church. Not because there was a mass, but because there was the clock. Yes, that life-saving clock, which played the melody at 12. Listening to this organ music became such a significant daily task. So important that I would feel like I was committing a sin if I missed this ritual, thereby I would eventually fail to finish the thesis. Sometimes I could not finish my planned work by noon. Then I still, in the middle of writing, rushed into the church for the 12 o'clock melody. When the music ended, I prayed. 'Please give me strength. Please . . . '

In the afternoon, I usually did reading. Or I revised my writing. Or I did something that did not require a high level of concentration: for example, making and checking a bibliography. And importantly, I watched dramas or films that were related to my thesis or situation in one way or another. Not necessarily because I wanted to take a break, but rather because I wanted to keep motivated. So I carefully selected: movies based on true events, works describing tormented but motivated characters and some sad features. While I was watching those stories, almost all the time, I shed tears. The key point here: those tears cleansed my mind, getting me inspired.

Sometime between 4 and 5 p.m., I had an early dinner. Then another short walk. Now, I began to write again. This time however not in the office, but on the street—writing the thesis in my head while running. I organised and reorganised a structure of the thesis. I revised what I had written in the morning. I thought about how to strengthen a weak part of the thesis. Some valuable ideas and new terms also came up during running. Back to the office building, I took a shower. Then I usually wrote a research diary: the thoughts I had while running, or some other things about the thesis. After this I did some reading until I got sleepy. I loved that dizzy feeling. It meant I had finished my planned work and lived through the day fully. That made me happy. Before I took off and locked the door, I said to my office. 'Thank you very much. See you tomorrow.' Yes, to the office. Because my office was my best friend.

All the above was possible, as I was able to use a single office in the twenty-four seven (seven days a week) building, where a shower room was also available to use. How grateful and lucky I was. On the way to my room, while walking, I briefly outlined what to write on the following day. At home I washed up, then went to bed sometime between 8 and 9. Oh, do not forget. I prayed again before I closed the eyes. With the dizzy feeling after running and the shower, I then fell into a deep sleep. One last thing. Sometimes I even had a dream about the thesis. Ideally, that was how I spent my whole day. That was how I survived one day after another.

During those days, I thought that I was living like a mayfly. 'My lifespan is one day. If I can finish one part of the thesis, I'm done. That's my day. Then I would die when I go to bed. The next morning, I would be reborn. Then another twenty-four hours. Again, let's do one thing. Yes, just one thing. That's enough.' This way of thinking gave me some comfort. Everything will be over today. Only twenty-four hours. Nothing more, nothing less. That is it. Be simple—only one thing. Knowing that my life would be over in twenty-four hours gave me a mysterious strength. It was this awareness of a symbolic death that kept me moving forward. Worrying about, even thinking about tomorrow could be too much. You put every energy, every effort on today. Then die, and a new life. Again die, and another life . . .

Often I woke up around midnight or 1 a.m., which meant I just slept for four hours or so. If possible, however, I went to the office right away. I had just one thing in mind. I knew that I could concentrate better in the very early morning, so I started to write. Most likely, I then became tired much earlier than usual. And the rest of the day was almost thrown away. Still, I was satisfied. I had done, no matter how small it was, one part of the thesis already. 'Remember. The day exists only for one purpose—the thesis,' I said to myself.

It was like doing a marathon. The only way to finish your marathon is to keep running until the very end. No matter how slow you are, no matter how long it takes, you keep going. There are no other options. Of course, you could quit if necessary. But as far as you want to finish the marathon, you just go, until the end. And there is one quick secret. Let's say you run the full marathon course. It is a long distance. From the very beginning if you think you should run about 42 km, you may feel, 'That's too long.' Something far away. Particularly if you run the full course for the first time, it becomes a bit difficult to imagine how to do it. And you may want to give up already. If you, however, divide the full course into small parts, it would become a different story. For example, you might want to think you run 10 km only—much shorter than 42 km. Now you just focus on 10 km. It would make you feel much closer. And hopefully, it would ease your tension. Then, imagine that you run this short course several times. In other words, instead of thinking that you need to run 42 km from the beginning, and that you feel exhausted even before you start, please try to think that you run *just* 10 km, four times. That way, hopefully you would be able to sustain yourself. By taking on one by one, you would become more focused.

Of course, sometimes, it was not as simple as that. I did not feel strong enough. I could not go up the stairs in the office building. On several occasions, I even had to stop while going down the stairs. Then I sighed deeply, 'This is not living . . .' Apart from my own mayfly, it was like my lifespan was becoming shorter day by day. But I even used to think that I would be honoured to get sick while writing the thesis. 'Working hard like a machine . . . if this could help me finish the PhD, if it could get me closer to the finish line of the project, I wouldn't care much about my body—if my body aches, it's an honour for me.' In retrospect, it was a dangerous and very arrogant thought. If I had seriously fallen ill before, could I still think like that? And what if I had really fallen ill while I was working? Back then, however, I meant it. Indeed, my eyesight had already been deteriorating since the beginning of my final year. It started quite abruptly. Yes, literally, so suddenly . . . Unlike before, everything within a certain range looked blurry. My stomach felt hollow with fear. My eyes more or less remained as such . . . So what if my eyes had got far worse? Could I still keep writing and finishing the thesis?

Actually when I was working on my very first book about the case, based on the MA thesis, I got sick. It was right after I sent a draft manuscript to a publisher. I had been relatively healthy and had no serious illness at all. But the following day after the submission, out of the blue I felt sick and would remain unwell for about a week. I was slightly scared, because it was so sudden. Powerlessly lying on the floor at home, I whispered. 'Uhhh . . . Maybe this shows how difficult it is to work on the case of KAL . . . This tragedy, this pain and the still missing 115 people . . . If this is a price to pay for dealing with all those things, it's okay. I can embrace this. It's my honour . . . Uhhh . . . '

At the writing-up stage of my PhD, when things did not go well, I constantly recalled Coelho's (2003: 171) words: 'when you want something, all the universe conspires in helping you to achieve it.' Here, my question was 'you.' In 'when you want something,' who are *you*? That was because I felt like someone wanted me to give up. So, that *someone* became *you* there. The flip side of Coelho's words: when someone wants you to *fail*, all the universe conspires in helping that someone to achieve it. Think of it. The entire universe is operating against you—because of someone's wishes. That however sharpened my spirit. 'Okay. Someone wants me to stop. And I am working against that someone's full force of universe. Why? Because that someone is afraid of me finishing this thesis. Why? Because what I am doing is meaning-ful. Why? Because no one has ever done it. Now, I *want*, more sincerely. I work, harder. So I will make *that universe* turning towards me, conspiring in helping *me* to finish the thesis.'

Then the result? You might want to ask Erzsébet Strausz (2018: 1, empha-sis in original): when the work was finished, 'it was simply a miracle that it was *there*.' I passed the thesis with no corrections. And the focus of my viva, was already on how to turn the thesis into a book.

* * *

15 January 2013, Munhwa Broadcasting Corporation (MBC). The date, 15 January, is special when it comes to the case of KAL 858. The government released the official findings of the case on this day. Far away from Korea, I typed 'KAL 858' on the web and looked over its search results. One news report caught up my eye: Kim's special interview programme was scheduled to be on air tonight from 11:15 p.m. This timeslot was originally for another regular programme, but MBC suddenly changed the schedule in the morning. As before, I knew that it would be quite disturbing to see Kim on the televi-sion. I however felt obliged to watch the programme later.

'That was a meeting in which I apologised to the families of the victims and sought reconciliation. It was heart-breaking. We cried together, and shook hands,' said Kim (MBC 2013). She was indicating that it was never easy. 'It was very hard. Although people say time is the best healer, I again sincerely apologise, because I gave them extreme pain. [. . .] In fact, it was not easy for me to see those families.' Kim gently nodded her head several times. It appeared that she was parched with thirst. By the way, she wrote books and met them with royalties. Kim also described that moment. 'Yes, because that was the only thing I could do . . . ' She stressed this part with her hand gesture. 'We each other . . . were really saddened by our fate . . . We burst into a lot of tears.' The presenter said that Kim's eyes were a bit wet now. The presenter then looked downwards, as if he was saying something very hard himself.

The programme lasted for about one hour. The presenter tried to wrap up the programme by asking Kim whether she had any message for the families of the victims. 'Yeah . . . well, in fact it was not easy for me to come to this place today. But . . . today 15 January is . . . on 15 January in 1988 there was my first press conference,' Kim began in a quiet voice while mostly look-ing downwards. 'And . . . in 2003 once the Roh Moo-hyun government was launched, regarding this case, there were occasions at the governmental level to frame it as a fake, for example by saying that it was a fake, it was fabricated,' Kim kept saying in a relatively quiet voice. 'But in this attempt, not only the government organisations got involved but also terrestrial broadcasting joined in . . . ' The presenter lowered his head when Kim mentioned broadcasting. 'And PD Notebook *from MBC was also deeply involved. So . . . I wanted to take this opportunity to, again, deeply apologise to the families of the deceased.'*

The presenter looked at Kim with a serious look on his face. Kim continued to say that she was alive because she was the witness to the case. 'And, I am grateful to MBC for being courageous today . . . Well, I want not only MBC but also other broadcasting companies like Korean Broadcasting System (KBS) and Seoul Broadcasting System (SBS), along with the government organisations and other groups, to be courageous as such.' Kim lowered her head and slightly gulped as soon as she finished, as if she had said something too much.

The presenter thanked Kim. A picture of the wreckage of KAL 858 was shown as a background image on a big screen behind him. He began to wrap up. The camera showed the photo of Kim's wedding in the centre. 'As much as we can, we'd like to hope that this programme would serve not as the place to unintentionally offer another excuse for the dispute, but as the first step towards genuine reconciliation and forgiveness. This is the end of today's programme.'

I closed my eyes. After taking a few minutes of rest, I stood up and went out for a walk. Most of all, I could not stop asking, 'Why now?' Just four weeks ago, I was deeply frustrated by the result of the presidential election in South Korea. Park Geun-hye, the daughter of the former military dictator Park Chung-hee, had won the election. The still incumbent President Lee Myung-bak, who reversed most of the two previous liberal governments' policies and therefore was responsible for various disastrous consequences, would be succeeded by Park Geun-hye.

One of the most infamous actions that Lee had taken was to control the media. He and his government, had almost forcefully, replaced chiefs of some major media companies with people who shared their political orientations. These media outlets included MBC, KBS and Yonhap Television News (YTN); the government or government-related agencies had substantial influence on the operations of these companies as the biggest shareholder. Labour unions protested by going on strike and many journalists were fired. Not surprisingly, the government had to face a huge wave of the public outcries. President Lee, however, pushed forward into the controversial entrance of the chaos. It was no wonder why Lee's nickname was the Bulldozer. *He seemed determined to bulldoze every legacy left by the two liberal presidents*

Kim Dae-jung and Roh Moo-hyun. Many people feared that Park as the new driver would accelerate this action. Considering that her inauguration was a month away, MBC's sudden decision to broadcast Kim's interview may have had something to do with this political climate.

As to the interview itself, I had many questions. First, Kim's description of the meeting between her and the families of KAL was problematic. According to Kim, the reconciliatory meeting went well. The families seemed to understand and forgive Kim. And they all cried together. In 2009, during my interview with a family member of KAL 858, I could hear a very different account of the gathering and what had happened afterwards.

The Agency for National Security Planning [ANSP, the current NIS] people brought Hyunhee Kim to the meeting place. There were seven of us representing the family association. When they entered the place, I asked her to come to me. I told her to sit next to me and held her hand with my left hand. I . . . my hand was shivering, but her hand was motionless. You know, she must have been scared so her hand should be shaking, but that's not the case . . . And I said: 'You must not marry. You made all of us widows.' I don't know why I said this, but I said that she should not marry. But I wasn't aware that she was going to marry soon. We met in December and in early January, a newspaper said that she had married. So what happened? She was already preparing to marry, the ANSP finished all the preparation to get her married and arranged the meeting! The wedding date was already set, but I didn't know that and said, 'You should not marry.' And I asked her to live with a grandmother who lost her son because of the case. She said yes, but now, she was going to marry . . . So I was really angry, so angry that I felt like I was going to die. Really, you know, this Republic of Korea fooled commoners like us, the powerless people. How dare you! (Interview, Duksoon Choo, 8 August 2009)

This family did not stop there. 'When I said that she should not marry, she replied yes. Then I said, "Sign a written promise." I gave her a paper and a pencil and said, "Because just saying yes is not enough, give us a written promise!" So she wrote something with her hand . . . She was forced to write.' That is, the mood of the gathering was different from what Kim described. There was a lot of tension. And only seven families out of 115 managed to meet Kim. Importantly, this meeting was arranged by the intelligence agency right before Kim got married, which angered those families. From Kim's words only, no one could know anything like this. Kim also said that she voluntarily delivered her book royalties to the families. I heard a rather different account of the event. The same family member above recounted: 'We thought that she had come to the meeting to give us her book royalties—we didn't know that she was going to marry after giving this money! We just thought that she was giving the money to poor families.' According to Kim, the donation seemed to be made purely out of the goodness of her heart. But from this family's view, it was like a deal: Take this money. In return, please be quiet when you hear the news that I married . . . Again, no one could know anything like this from Kim's interview.

About the Roh Moo-hyun government, I strongly disagreed with what Kim said. Overall, Kim seemed to be very upset about the reinvestigation efforts. She took it as the vicious attempt to make her a fake. But that was not right. The key point here: there have been substantial and widespread questions concerning what really happened to KAL 858. No dead bodies were found, no black box either. The official search operation lasted for only ten days. Then the suspect, who mysteriously survived her suicide attempt, brought to South Korea. It was just one day before the immensely important presidential election. The following day, a candidate from the military government's ruling party became the winner. Without physical evidence, based only on the suspect's statements, the government hastily released the official findings. Now the criminal was sentenced to death, but just fifteen days later she became a free citizen. In addition, questions including various contradictions within her confession and the intelligence agency's manipulations remained unanswered. She then married a secret agent and disappeared.

Now, taken all together: Should everyone just believe what the government said? Should everyone trust Hyunhee Kim? If the government had explained clearly enough, if Kim had been honest about her confession, it would have been a different story. But what happened? The government was busy with using the case in the presidential election. It was called 'Operation Rainbow,' led by the intelligence agency: the military government and the spy agency controlled the media and organised mass demonstrations to collect as many conservative votes as possible. Kim published several books based on her still problem-ridden confession. What is more, it later turned out that the books were actually written by a ghost writer commissioned by the spy agency. Given all this, anyone with common sense could pose questions. The reinvestigation was necessary.

* * *

I got an email from the Dean of College's personal assistant.

'The Dean has requested a thirty-minute meeting with you to discuss your role in the Department. Could you kindly advise of any availability you may have?' Almost out of blue, I did not know why I got this message. Furthermore, why Dean of College?—not Head of School, nor Head of Department, but Dean? Indeed, it was strange. I asked back. 'With all due respect, if I may, this message sounds a bit confusing . . . Just to clarify, allow me to ask you some quick questions please: 1) As I have never expected a meeting with Dean, could you briefly tell me why this meeting needs to be arranged please? 2) I wonder if *every* staff member of my Department has been invited to the meeting individually or if this meeting is specifically arranged for me.' While waiting for the reply, I began to suspect this might have something to do with my resignation. Nothing else could be. Well, I got the answer. According to the message, the Dean wanted to have an informal talk with me as he had heard good things about me but had also heard that I have resigned. The message said that I was more than welcome to decline the meeting.

Yes, as I guessed. But I never expected that the Dean would have been interested in my resignation. I wondered how to respond to the Dean's request. If there would be a meeting, I would inevitably talk about problems that led me to quit. In one way or another, no matter how politely put, this could be taken as criticism against my Department and School. Yes, there were some issues, *as in any other place*. I would never say this was unique to my case. Most of all, I was still grateful to have had an opportunity to work, having been a professor. Just because I was leaving, I would not betray this gratitude, my colleagues and Department. No.

Speaking of which, one of the concerns I had was my departure might have a negative impact on the Department's operation next year. Indeed, to minimise this potential damage, I submitted a notice of leave four months before my anticipated formal departure—much earlier than the University regulation said. I did not have to do it. This advanced notice however would allow the Department to recruit my substitute as soon as possible. I did not want to do any harm. So, I replied. 'Most of all, I am truly honoured to hear that the Dean heard some positive things about me. And I am flattered to be invited to a meeting. But if I may, hearing this wonderful message and the invitation itself are very encouraging and enough for me . . . Thank you so much indeed. I sincerely and strongly hope that the University's support for the Department will continue.'

How to say goodbye is important—more important than how to say hi. I wrote a thank-you card for each one of my unit members. I also bought a small gift for everyone. After all, they were good colleagues and kind people. Some of them often included a brief note in their email to other colleagues. 'Hope we all survive!' Yes, I genuinely hoped that they would survive well. Thank you all. And my students: I was really grateful to them for accepting me as a teacher and friend. And I was truly sorry for leaving. 'Huhhh . . . ' I sighed deeply before I started to write a group email to students. 'It makes me sad to announce that I am leaving the University . . . I wish I could have done more for you. Importantly, I would like to thank you for your cooperation. I wholeheartedly wish you all the best for your future studies. Many thanks & take care . . . ' I was grateful, and sorry. As a small token of this feeling, I wanted to do something special. I made a modest donation to the students' association of my Department. I could not tell the whole story about why I decided to resign. I just wanted them to know that I cared for them. I did not want them to misunderstand—'He's leaving because he didn't care for us.' No, not in any way at all. Hope our paths will come across again. Goodbye all.

Before I left, I also wanted to look around my classrooms—places full of the scent of my passion and sweat. I had always tried to do my best. 'Yes, let's say goodbye to them as well.' The first room. I slowly surveyed the classroom, from the left to right, from the front to back. Then I started to walk through. I gently touched things: the teacher's computer, whiteboard and students' desks. I sat down on a chair in the middle of the room and closed my eyes. Further, I placed my hands together as if I were praying. 'Thank you so much, thank you,' I whispered. Then I put down my head, kissed the desk. I repeated this goodbye-ceremony in the rest of my classrooms. And my office building. I walked through the corridors. Memorable places there— my troubled shared office for four where I had stayed upon my arrival, the first-aid-kit room which served as my temporary secret garden and various rooms of my colleagues.

And last but not least, coming back to my single office, the *safe haven.* A small space without any luxury furniture—but a deep sanctuary that had helped me survive so far. I thanked this office by performing a Korean style big bow. I raised both hands to my chest, bent both knees to kneel, placed both hands on the floor, then bent my upper body and bowed my head. 'You meant everything to me. Thank you.'

Still, leaving my job itself forced me to reflect on lots of things. Most of all, it did not mean that I just gave up everything. I needed time—my own time not to be squeezed, my time to breathe and think. Again, it was a bit like running a marathon. One important thing is to do it at your own pace. If you run fast, just because others do, you would easily get out of breath. And if you keep doing this, it would ruin your marathon, it would ruin you eventually. If you lose your pace, you lose your happiness. This was what troubled me. Becoming more and more cynical, I felt that I was losing myself. To stop this, on YouTube, I often typed words such as 'sad movies,' 'sad videos' or 'touching videos.' With tears, I felt a bit better. Sometimes, I just put my hands on my chest. Literally to feel my heart, to listen to my heart. I did not want to become cold. Of course, some people envied me. I was a professor with a relatively stable income. Again, I was really grateful. Particularly in the Korean context, becoming a professor has been traditionally regarded as a big deal. Leaving aside this, I had food to eat, clothes to wear and a room to live in. 'What's the matter with you?' someone might ask. 'Look around the world. For example, refugees. Do you know how many people are in dire situations?' I might need to feel ashamed.

But, I also knew: If you are unhappy, you will make others unhappy. If you are not happy, the world does not look happy . . . I was becoming like a machine. I did something, because I was instructed. I did other things, because of my duty. To be fair, compared with other sectors like business and industry, I was aware that one could enjoy a relatively high level of freedom and autonomy in academia. One may add that these days, in the age of neoliberalism and fierce competition, universities are becoming more like commercial companies. Still, academics enjoy some privileges. To me, this unfortunately did not matter that much. The urgent problem was that I was suffocating here. I tried to bite the bullet. But the suffocation came on and on. It became a matter of survival.

On the other hand, to some extent, I wanted to become *desperate* again—in a positive sense, doing things out of a deep desire and out of desperation. I wanted to go back to the days when I was not a professor. I recalled the days when I was writing my thesis. They were hard times. But I could embrace them, because there was a meaning to pursue. A very tough time there. As long as there is a meaning, however, you can endure it. That is a positive force of desperation. Something was there, deep inside me—something that tried to give me a wake-up call. Before it was too late, I decided to take that call.

Accommodating that call led me to go to another university. I was not a professor anymore. I did not get a salary. I did not receive any funding. But I just went there. My top priority now: to finish a book project that had been postponed for several years. The book I had always desired. The project I, however, could not proceed. The mission I designed out of the case of KAL 858, which changed my life enormously. And something that made me decide to resign as a professor.

The new place was located in an area surrounded by trees. It almost looked like a cottage. At first sight, I fell in love with the place. This is a good sign, I thought. My new home, a dormitory, had a problem though. In principle, there was no bed; and no desk either. I initially took this unexpected inconvenience as an opportunity—an opportunity to keep me tense, hungry and desperate. Think about, for instance, the families of the missing of KAL 858. Not knowing whether their loved ones were actually dead or not, not knowing the whole truth of the case, their suffering has been immense for thirty years. And look at me. Considering those families, my situation could not be compared in any way at all. Nevertheless, while writing the book, sleeping in the room with no bed would constantly remind me of their uncomfortable circumstances. Yes, I planned to sleep on the floor. But a little twist here. Although I did not ask for anything, an almost-bed-like mattress was provided. Much better than none. Fortunately, and *unfortunately*, my plan to sleep on a hard floor was scrapped. But it made me realise that I was ready to devote myself to KAL 858 and the book project.

* * *

8 March 2014, Seoul. South Korean people also celebrated International Women's Day. This year's events were more special, because Park Geun-hye entered the Blue House as the first woman president of South Korea in 2013. Special . . . not because Korea had a female leader, but because her presidency triggered various controversies over gender politics. From the beginning of her presidential campaigns, when she claimed that it was time for a woman to become a president, not many people believed that she was entitled to say so. Most of her political assets were derived from her father's legacy, the military general Park Chung-hee's rule for about twenty years. As a politician, she had not done anything particular for women's rights and gender equality. So it was not surprising when many feminist activists and scholars accused her of stealing benefits of feminist movements. Unfortunately, as Park's presidency just marked its first anniversary, South Korean feminists were proved right. So, many more debates and thoughts for this year. I began to look through the news reports about special events.

Then one breaking news came to my attention: Malaysia Airlines Flight 370 disappeared with 239 people. This was immensely disturbing news. Such news always reminded me of KAL 858. In ten days, I would face another disturbing news on 17 March. One news channel called News Y announced that to discuss the Malaysian flight case they would invite a very special expert . . . Hyunhee Kim.

'This case of the disappearance of Malaysia Airlines is a mystery. The bomber of KAL, Ms Hyunhee Kim. I wonder what she thinks. So we invited her to come to our studio,' the presenter bowed (News Y 2014). Kim answered in a quiet voice and bowed as well. The presenter asked Kim what she thought about the case. After a brief silence, Kim said. 'Well, up until now, nothing has been recovered . . . well . . . now, Malaysia is investigating. But it is said that it doesn't seem to be a terror, rather it could be a hijacking.' 'A hijacking is in fact a terror,' interrupted the presenter. 'Yeah, it is part of terror attacks. So it seems many think that this could be a hijacking.'

The presenter and Kim discussed various possibilities. When it came to a perpetrator's claim of responsibility, Kim said the following. 'By the way, looking at this case of Malaysia Airlines, well . . . it's a little bit different. North Korea has always been . . . take the case of the sinking of the Cheonan corvette. Although clearly there was a North Korean marking on the recovered propeller, which read "No. 1" [. . .] they laid all the responsibility on South Korea.' Kim went on to say that the case of KAL was the same. 'Although I was ordered to do it, [. . .] they still don't admit it. And also, in accordance with North Korea's instruction, in South Korea the Jongbuk [pro-North Korean] faction still say things like, well, the case is a fake, right? That's exactly what North Korea intended.' The interview lasted for about twelve minutes.

As before, Kim appearing on the television itself was disturbing to me. But I still watched the programme—although I did not want to, I felt I had to. Among the issues Kim mentioned, I found one thing especially problematic: the case of the Cheonan. A South Korean naval ship was sunk on 26 March 2010. I happened to be in Seoul to do my fieldwork. The South Korean government immediately claimed that the ship had been destroyed by North Korea. Forty-six sailors were killed. The next day, I went to a small restaurant for lunch. An anchor was delivering the news about the sinking on the television. The owner of the restaurant shouted. 'See . . . North Korea did it again! What a bastard!'

On 20 May, the first day of the June local election campaigns, the Joint Civilian-Military Investigation Group supported the government's claim and concluded that North Korea had killed the soldiers. Crucial evidence was the Korean marking 'No. 1' that Kim had mentioned. But this official result has been challenged by a number of questions, such as contradictions within witness statements, the authorities' manipulation of video recording evidence and scientific controversy over explosive materials. One opinion poll in September 2010 suggested that only 32.5 per cent of the South Korean population trusted the official findings (E-News 2010).

Along with the controversial questions, North Korea denied its involvement. Four years on, the case of the Cheonan was still going on. Kim said that this case looked similar to the case of KAL 858. In a quite different context, I also thought that the Cheonan resembled KAL 858. Let's see: Immediately after the incident, the South Korean authorities suspected North Korean involvement. This initial accusation was reflected in the official findings. North Korea denied any responsibility. Meanwhile many unanswered questions were raised . . . Whatever the truth, the case of the Cheonan, just like the case of KAL, was such a sad reminder of the divided Korea.

The same went for the so-called Jongbuk faction. Kim labelled the reinvestigation campaigners as the Jongbuk faction. The word itself, a derogatory term generally used to blame a person or a group for supporting or following North Korea's positions, should be examined carefully. Given the ongoing war and division, North Korea has long been regarded as the enemy state in South Korea. Everything about North Korea has become something to be denied or defeated. If you were called Reds (communists or someone who supports North Korea) or Jongbuk by others, your political/social life would be in big trouble. This magic word and the politics surrounding it became institutionalised, most notably, through the National Security Law. Another sad reminder of the divided Korea.

I would not say that only the South has this problem—the North has its own version of this magic word. But I do not know much about North Korea. At least as a South Korean, I know that this security mindset has a long history in the South. Probably the seed of McCarthyist politics was planted in 1945, when Korea was liberated from Japan and the ideological conflict between the Left and Right over the power vacuum began to emerge. The division of the Korean peninsula in 1948 intensified the conflict. For example, tens of thousands of innocent people on Jeju Island were killed by the government forces and right-wing militias during the first South Korean government, the Syngman Rhee regime. To make matters worse, the subsequent Korean War consolidated this deeply divisive political landscape. General Chun Doo-hwan's Kwangju massacre in 1980 was also in this line of McCarthyism.

The violent Cold War–style witch hunt is still going on in various ways. I myself have been a victim since I joined the families of KAL 858 in demanding the reinvestigation. The defenders of the official findings called people like me Jongbuk. The reason was simple—as North Korea denied its responsibility, demanding the reinvestigation would benefit North Korea. Therefore, you must have been instructed by North Korea . . . Now, even Kim used this magic word, Jongbuk.

* * *

I, now the recently resigned professor, began to settle into my new university and department. A semester just started and the orientation meeting for students was arranged. I was not an official member of staff, but I had also been invited to introduce myself to students. It was refreshing. And this reminded me of my time as a baby teacher.

The orientation meeting, my very first semester as assistant professor. All students and all teachers gathered. It was a general information session. Teachers introduced themselves to students and briefly talked about the courses they would teach. Importantly, as a new member of staff, it was the very first opportunity for me to meet students. It was about two weeks since I had arrived. A new country, new people. Although I had visited earlier for my job interview, everything was new to me—not to mention students whom I had never met. For me, it was absolutely important to make a good start with them. I thought a lot about this gathering: how to introduce myself and what to say about my class. One course after another, the relevant teacher stood up. And now, my turn. 'Hello. My name is Sungju Park-Kang. Nice to meet you.' At that moment, I was interrupted by applause from students. I said something very simple, very basic. Nothing special . . . except that I did it in a local language. That was how I first met students as a professor. And that applause gave me the courage I needed.

The similar thing would impress me at the same meeting in the following semester. Because the message about the meeting was a bit unclear, I missed the first part of the gathering, which I should have attended. When my office phone rang loudly, I realised that something was wrong. How embarrassing. The students and teachers were waiting for me. Especially thinking of the students, I was so sorry. Can you guess what they did when I entered the meeting room? Students applauded—what welcomed me was not their exhausted faces from a long wait, but their applause. Yes, it seemed that students liked me. I liked them too.

Sometimes things happen abruptly though. It was one of the presentation sessions. Students delivered their presentations in turn. I watched them and took brief notes. Feedback including grades would be provided in two weeks. Nothing complicated. What was tricky at the time was that my mind was elsewhere. I could not focus on the presentations. Why? Sometime around 29 November each year, I always become vigilant. It is the memorial day of the case of KAL 858. I have my own way to commemorate this important day: I write and publish an annual article before 29 November each year. I usually publish it through an online newspaper. That year was no exception. I finished the article somewhat late though. I managed to send it to the media on 28 November, just one day before the memorial day. To be more precise: right before my class started. So literally I had to rush into the classroom.

The presentation session began. I took a seat and started to observe the presentations. But I was still thinking about the article I had just finished and sent. The session went on anyway. Before I dismissed the class, one of the presenters asked me if I had any comments on today's presentations. As I was supposed to give formal feedback sometime later, I did not quite answer the question, politely. But that student insisted. It was a bit of an odd situation. Some presentations were good and some were bad. And each presentation had its own strength and weakness. I did not want to specifically identify those things—some students might be embarrassed in public.

However, I could not just ignore the demand anymore. So I started my answer with something like: 'Well, some presentations were well-researched and some were not. And . . . ' And . . . ? Well, and . . . ? Suddenly, my mind went blank. I could not continue. Silence . . . A very awkward moment in front of students. Then, another presenter asked a question. 'What do you think of my presentation?' 'Well, I am not an expert on your topic today, but . . . ' I could not continue again. Silence . . . Again, an awkward moment. And that silence was broken by the first questioner. 'I think your presentation was . . . ' A specific comment followed. While listening to this answer, I became so ashamed. 'You are better than me. Thank you,' I said to the first questioner. Then I dismissed the class. What a nightmare. I sank through the floor. Deep down there, I did not want to come out. I did not know how to face the students next time.

Deep inside me, I had to admit something. If I had paid full attention to students' presentations, I might have been able to answer the questions. Partly the problem was caused by the article I had to write. After all, I thought that all this was down to the case of KAL 858. I decided to take that embarrassment as a price to pay for my devotion to the case. Yes, sometimes one gets hurt by something that one deeply cares about. The following day, on 29 November, a little surprise happened. My writing became the most read article on that newspaper, and it retained the first spot for a few more days. My most successful article came out at the expense of my most embarrassing moment in teaching ever.

At the same time, I wondered if I was just trying to make an excuse. Remember: although it was late, I had managed to send the article before the session. Job done. Now I could, and importantly had to focus on the presentations. But why had I still been thinking about the article? It was me that did not do the job, not the case of KAL 858. Yes, it was me. I was the problem. I could not focus? Maybe I did not want to focus. Do not put the blame on KAL 858. It was simple—I was not brave enough to admit it. I was not honest. In response to this inner voice, I drooped my head. I did not know what to say. I was ashamed, just ashamed.

'But still . . . ' I mumbled to myself. What? 'Still . . . if it had not been about KAL 858, I would not have had written something from the very beginning.' There you go, again! 'Huhhh . . . I don't know. I, I just don't know.' I now became confused. 'I don't want to struggle. I want peace.' Yes, you do not have to struggle. You want to be happy. You want something more pleasant. 'If I hadn't met the case, if I hadn't worked on the case . . . ' Yes, you do not want to get exhausted. 'If I had followed the government's demand, if I hadn't refused to revise my thesis . . . ' Yeah, it is all down to you. You made a wrong choice. 'I wish KAL 858 had never come to me. I wish none of this had happened . . . '

At that moment, something came into my mind: 'So do all who live to see such times, but that is not for them to decide. All we have to decide is what to do with the time that is given to us.' So exhausted that I was almost falling asleep. I stretched myself. While yawning, I could see the DVD set of *The Lord of the Rings* on my bookcase. I bought it after I finished the PhD. It was my own gift to myself. Along with other characters, on its cover, there were Frodo and Gandalf . . .

Oh, and this reminded me of another thing that I did around that time. I briefly went back to Korea; I was invited to present my thesis at the memorial ceremony of the case of KAL 858. It coincided with the twenty-fifth anniversary. Before I left Korea again, I met my very special friend. We talked about my thesis. It was probably when I mentioned something about the separation between myself and the case—the researcher and the researched. Next to us, there was a campaign banner of one presidential candidate. The candidate was from the opposition party running for the presidential election in 2012. A former human rights lawyer, he was the closest staff, dearest colleague and lifelong friend of the ex-president Roh Moo-hyun, who tragically died. The candidate appeared to be struggling to separate himself from the late Roh. I thought that I could almost see myself in this candidate. Maybe, I was more serious than the candidate. Maybe the other way around.

One thing was clear though. I felt I was so immersed in the case—too immersed to get out. People warned me that I needed to maintain some distance from the subject. It was friendly advice, which I myself acknowledged. But from a certain point, I had been struggling to know how to do it. After the PhD, I expected I would feel differently. But I did not. I feared that I would never be able to get away from the case. I was stuck; I was imprisoned—a life sentence. It was that moment when I burst into tears, making my friend perplexed. I was afraid. I did not know how to endure that life sentence.

Once I said goodbye to the friend, I took a walk, a long walk. It was already night. A dark and cold December. I had not burst into such a flood of tears since my father passed away when I was a teenager. I would never forget those tears, and that cold December. Then what happened next? I decided to accept the life sentence. I decided to take it as my fate. Yes, a destiny. It sounds old-fashioned; it sounds too heavy. But that was what I felt. 'Let's go until the end. I don't know what would be there. I don't know who would be waiting there. I know, however, that this is what I want. Yes, let's go until the end—till the very end.' I could be wrong. I could suffocate myself. But after all, like Gandalf said, 'All we have to decide is what to do with the time that is given to us.'

Not surprisingly this conviction was reflected in my post-PhD life: namely, my teaching and research. I believed that a strong motivation was most important in academic endeavours, like in any other activities. I particularly emphasised this aspect of learning to students. 'My priority task as a teacher is not transferring knowledge. It needs to be about awakening students' own motivations. And to help them stay motivated,' I said to myself. When I received an email one month after I had become a professor, it seemed that at least some students understood what I meant.

'As part of my journalism course assignment, I am required to interview a scholar on their work. My fellow classmates have told me passionately about your class and research. So when I received the assignment, I immediately thought of you.' I was genuinely surprised, and truly honoured . . . It meant a lot to me. 'Thank you very much for your email. What a nice surprise! It is very humbling to read your message. I am sure that there are much more qualified scholars than me . . . But if you want, yes, let me be part of your interview project. Wow, it makes me nervous!' This student asked me various questions, among others, about: my PhD thesis, what research meant to me, the most important aspect of academic research and my future plans for research. The interview request from the student made me think that I was on the right track. And I was really grateful to students. I wanted to do better for them.

In the same semester, other students put me in a different situation. Just a third of students attended the class at some point. 'Finally has my worry become reality?' I asked myself. This course was designed by another teacher and the same teacher was supposed to run. But due to unforeseen circumstances, I took it over. I was only familiar with some part of subjects. I however had had no choice. Unfortunately, that meant I was not as prepared as I should have been. It was important for me to be honest with students. So I explained this background at the opening session, and told students. 'I will try to do my best. Let's learn together.' Yes, I tried. Otherwise the eventual victims would be students. But sometimes I myself was not satisfied. Then, that day came. I naturally thought this huge absence was caused by me. I would not blame the students.

'Welcome everyone. Thank you for coming. Well, as you can see, we have only a few people here today. As a teacher of this course, I think I need to take responsibility. I am sorry . . . ' Some students shook their heads. 'No, it's not your fault,' one student said. At the same time, I wanted to keep trying and doing better. That was because still there were others.

One week before the last teaching session of the semester. I was busy and could not prepare enough for the session for one of my courses. What a shame. Me in front of the class. 'Welcome everyone. As usual, thank you for coming. And I'd like to start with . . . ' 'Excuse me!' One student interrupted. She then came straight towards me. I was alerted. There was something in her hand. 'As today is our last session, let's start the session with a little surprise. We'd like to thank you for your teaching and caring about us. And we prepared this. Thank you!' It was a present, wrapped up neatly. A total surprise. 'Ah . . . I don't know what to say . . . Wow. Thank you. Thank you so much! I really appreciate it.' That was all I could say and do. That was partly because I had never expected a present from students. But more importantly, that was because my head was still busy with sorting out the ideas about how to do the session. I was more worried than pleased. I felt sorry . . .

Oh, and wait a minute . . . The last session? Suddenly I remembered that among the students there had been rumours about the semester ending one week earlier. But that was not true. Actually I clearly said in the syllabus that the last lesson would take place in the following week. For some reason, however, students misunderstood. 'Sorry, but just to make clear . . . I'm afraid that today is not the last session. I know that some other departments have their last sessions this week, but not our department. According to our syllabus, we will have the last session next week.'

Fortunately, that session went relatively well. Back to my office, I began to realise something—something about saying goodbye. I believed that I would have the last session with the students next week. The students believed that today was the last time. They were ready to say goodbye, but I was not. I thought about having more time with the students, but they did not. Although I *knew* that the class would end next week, although to some extent I was *ready*, I was still confused and surprised. Then what if I did not know at all? What if I was not ready at all? Think of that shock. Think of that frustration . . . A thought struck me. 'KAL 858 . . . The passengers suddenly disappeared. They were not ready at all. And their families neither. Without any prior notice, they had just gone. That was it. Just gone.' Yes, I was thinking about the case of KAL 858. Making connections between the surprise present, students' misunderstanding and the KAL case. Probably no one could imagine such a thing, except me. The opportunity to reflect on the suffering and shock of the missing passengers and their families—this was another totally unexpected present from students.

As to the original gift, out of sincere gratitude, I first kissed the wrapping. I cautiously observed the still unopened object and carefully removed the packaging. 'Ah . . . ' It was a vegetarian cooking book. At the beginning of the semester, I wanted to do something good for students. So I suggested an informal lunch gathering at my expense. We went to a local restaurant together. That was how students came to know that I was a vegetarian. And they remembered. How sweet of them. I kissed the cooking book. I was so honoured. Indeed, I was incredibly proud that students recognised my effort. After all, when it comes to teaching, students matter most—their reactions and feedback. And this gift represented that my teaching and I were positively received. As a baby professor, that was truly amazing. How to wrap up is always as important as how to get started. The following week, we had the actual last session. First I explained the Korean gift culture, in which the receiver does not open the present in front of the giver. That was why I did not open the present during class. And I described how I kissed the present. Students looked pleased. After this last session ended, one student asked me. 'Are you going to teach next semester as well?' I smiled.

The following semester. During one of the discussion sessions, the issue of demotivation was raised. It was when I emphasised the importance of motivation regarding writing a thesis. Indeed, I began my first session of this course by showing a video clip, without any explanation. Having made the classroom a little bit dark, I played the clip: a student was running around the playground. This character was a marathon runner and looked severely exhausted. His coach tried to stop him. But he kept running and finished one hundredth round, then collapsed. He was heavily out of breath. He however stood up, and put the coach's hand on his heart. Then the coach looked at him with wide-eyed surprise. The clip ended.

I finally spoke. 'This movie is called *Marathon*. The runner was circling the playground one hundred times, which his coach had jokingly instructed him to do. As you could see, when his coach later realised that he foolishly followed his instruction, the coach wanted to stop him. The thing is that the runner had a disability, a mental health issue. But he did what he could do and what he wanted to do. Like the clip showed, writing starts from your heart.' I put my hand on my chest. 'From here, your heart . . . ' I then added. 'Of course, you need some skills. There are some techniques to learn. We can do that together. But the thing is, when it comes to your heart, no one can help. Only you, you can do it—by yourself.'

Some weeks later when I briefly mentioned motivation again, one student said. 'I think *demotivation* is more important. Of course I want to write my thesis. But there are other things. I don't have much time. My other classes, minor course and so on. They discourage me.' Demotivation . . . A very useful word, I thought. 'First of all, I am so sorry to hear it. But yes, demotivation. You raised a very important issue. Yeah, that's quite difficult to deal with.' I meant it. You want to do something, but your circumstances do not allow you to do it. Even if you have a strong sense of motivation, if the surrounding conditions cannot support you, things crumble. I knew it from my own experience.

To have enough time to prepare for my job, I wanted to arrive at the University as early as possible—about one month before the semester started. But the job advertisement itself and the selection process ran a little behind schedule considering the academic calendar. Of course, I was sincerely grateful to get this job. Along with my visa application, however, the already late process led me to arrive two weeks before the opening of the semester. That was beyond my control. I now did not have much time. Adjusting to a new system, new people, new office, opening a bank account, finding a new room, making syllabi, various conflicting information on courses and regulations and so on. Everything was happening at the same time, with a tight schedule. All this made me exhausted even before my first session. In some ways, the classic question of individual agency and structure—individuals struggling in unfavourable environments.

Let's take a bank account. For some reason, the University, instead of me, needed to submit the required documents to the bank. And it took some time. When I went to the bank for my appointment, I was told that the University had not sent them the documents. With the bank's help, I called the University straight away and heard that the bank was right. I however learnt later that the University had sent the documents. In other words, it was the bank's mistake. I was so confused. When I went to the bank again and finally opened my account, it was already late. I had to collect my first salary directly at the University, by cash. I then went to the bank again, to pay that money into my account. I wasted a lot of energy and time.

My room was another example. Luckily, although it was very expensive, I secured a room before I arrived. But that was only for two weeks. After that, I had to find another place. Very fortunately, I was able to move to another room in the same house. But that was again only a temporary place. In two months, I would move again to a new place. I was grateful for finding the room itself, but moving already three times in less than three months caused enormous stress—ongoing insecurity until I found a new room one after another, and packing and unpacking again. Furthermore, my second room was directly exposed to the noisy street, so I often woke up around midnight or 1 a.m. It was not always easy to get back to sleep, and that almost ruined my days.

What about my office? I was told that I would have a temporary office first, and then get a permanent one later. I shared a temporary office with another member of staff. I was assistant professor with a heavy teaching load and responsibilities of thesis supervision. Naturally I wanted to get a permanent single office as soon as possible, at least before my first class. Although the teaching week was about to start, however, I had not heard anything about the office. I contacted the administration several times and heard that if I wanted to have a single office, I would need to move to another building. Otherwise, I had to stay in the temporary shared office. Thinking of my temporary room as well, that is my home, there would be so many moves going on. Not so easy, really.

Meanwhile there was a problem with my office computer as well. Its screen was too big. It easily caused eye strain. I contacted the IT service, but they did not have a smaller screen available. They just recommended me to consult the health-related service. Feeling disappointed, I visited the IT service in person. By chance, there I could see a smaller screen in use. The staff member in charge was sympathetic towards me and suggested a possibility of replacing that screen with my big one. This unusual and kind offer saved me.

Going back to my office. As I deeply wanted a single space, I decided to move. The decision was made, but locating a new office was another matter. It was not processed quickly enough. So I contacted, and also visited the administration. The timing was not so ideal. The administration itself was moving to a new venue and was caught up in its own business. Both sides were stressed, which eventually led to a little quarrel. Fortunately, the administration was also sympathetic. The following day, I was told that I had a single office at last. 'Thank you. Thank you so much!'

Okay, I now got the office. Then, it was time to actually move. There were a lot of books and documents—about ten boxes. In addition, my computer and the replaced screen. There were too many to carry by myself. To make matters worse, although the new building was not so far away from my temporary office, the way itself was a little tough. I had to cross a little bridge. So I considered asking the administration for help, but with going through the screen scandal and others, I did not want to make things complicated any further. In the end, I did it all alone. I went back and forth between the buildings several times. At some point, I was so burned out that I could not say any word when someone approached me and asked if I needed help—I just pretended not to see that kind person. That was how I managed to secure my own office in the middle of the semester. Moving to the new office turned out to be an incredibly significant decision. That single quiet space would serve as my little safe haven throughout my (unexpectedly) continuing struggles.

Several *incidents*, as I called them, followed. The issue of timetable change was one example. In the first semester, the secretariat told me that if teachers wanted, class timetables could change. Regarding one of my courses in the second semester, it appeared that such action was necessary. Around the end of the first semester, I contacted the secretariat and they indicated that it would be possible to accommodate my wishes. So I thought everything would be fine. As the opening of the new semester approached, however, I realised that the original timeslot was still on display to students. I contacted the secretariat and heard that they could not find an available classroom for the requested time. Well, the semester would start soon so it had to be worked out as early as possible. Otherwise, students could be very confused. And what if my requested change would lead to their timetable clashes? That was why I had already informed the secretariat of the change at the end of last semester.

Upon my plea, the secretariat said they would look into this again and get back to me with a new venue. I was waiting for the answer, but time was running out. When there was the orientation meeting with students one week before the first session, I asked them whether they knew the timetable. Their answer was the original timeslot, which meant the change was still not reflected in the displayed schedule. I quickly told students about the new timeslot. I then contacted the secretariat again. Unfortunately, the person in charge was away. So I had to explain everything again to another person. I then later heard that the change would not be possible, because no classroom was available.

With this belated confirmation, I quickly sent a group email to students saying that the class would start according to the original timetable. I now had to change my own plan as well—yes, I already organised my schedule based on the new timetable, which turned out not to be the case anymore. It was difficult to understand. If there were no available rooms, why did the secretariat not tell me in the first place? If I had known that the change was not possible from the beginning, things would have been much better. I would not have had to waste my time and energy. Students would not have had to be confused. A deep frustration overshadowed me. I, however, had no choice but to accept it. The following week: on my way to the first session, I could see several empty classrooms here and there. I felt like a fool. I still apologised to students for the confusion *I* caused. The next week: on my way to the second session, I could see empty classrooms again. Until the end of the semester, those rooms mostly remained empty.

Another matter was the grading sheets I received. I was supposed to record student's marks there, but they raised my eyebrows. For some reason, there were only a few students on the list. To make sure, I checked my email attachment again. Clearly it was an incomplete list. What did I do then? I just corrected it by myself. I cross checked all the students' names and added the missing ones to the list. On another occasion, a different teacher was listed as the course tutor—it should have been me. That different teacher originally planned to teach the course. The grading sheet however was not updated. These problems were not so serious compared to the timetable-change scandal. But those small things were big enough to make me become gradually unhappy.

I was aware that I was not the only one who had such feelings. Let's go back to my new office, where the back story is to be told. The administration made arrangements for me to collect a key. As instructed, I went to the maintenance office. They looked into a box where several keys were placed. And they said that they could not find anything about my office. I asked them to check again. 'No, nothing. Sorry.' I then went to the administration and explained the situation. The administrative staff looked confused and checked the record again. 'Yes, the key should be there!' Now, this administrative staff member headed to the maintenance office along with me. Then a little argument followed between this member of staff and the maintenance office. The maintenance team investigated the same box again. Strangely, the key turned up this time. On our way back, the administrative staff member complained about this mysterious event. 'Huhhh . . . A very confusing system!'

Yes, in that sense, I was not alone. And it was unfortunate. When those small and serious incidents recurred, my single office saved me. When various other issues troubled me, that quiet office comforted me. In this office, even eating became something meaningful. When I had a meal, more precisely when I was chewing food with closed eyes, things somehow felt calm. Like food was sliced into smaller pieces, my stress seemed to be sliced away. I became happy. Just like food being digested, my problems appeared to be digested in one way or another. I got energised again. Often music was added to this soul-searching activity. If I had stayed in a shared office, this almost meditation-like eating would not have been possible.

Sometimes, I went for a walk. There were many canals across the town. When I sat on my favourite bench and looked down at the waving water, I often thought. 'There are waves also inside me. Please let me stay in peace.' As sunshine was reflected in the water, making the water itself shiny, I wished. 'Please let my soul shine. Don't make me cynical.' I then would go back to my office, where I could concentrate again, where I became grateful again. 'Yes, at least, I have my own space.' That space was not so big, not so beautiful though—but big enough to accept myself, beautiful enough to lighten my burden.

Still, things can happen. I received an urgent email from the Head of Department. I was called into a meeting. 'There are complaints about your class.' The course in question was something that was not clearly defined who should teach from the beginning. Then it was agreed that I would lead the course. It was a thesis seminar. For a baby professor who had almost no experience in supervising theses, the course was a burdensome task. But I believed that I could utilise my own thesis writing experience. Indeed, when I got a student's interview request last semester, one of the questions was concerned with that experience.

Meanwhile, at the opening session, I conducted a quick survey about the difficulties students had with writing. Then along with my own programme, I covered those difficult areas each session. Sometimes I gave students a small piece of homework and discussed it together during the lesson. I thought that things were going relatively well. But what I heard at that urgent meeting was quite surprising: Some students were considering dropping the course, because they did not learn much from the course. They wanted something more specific. They wanted to discuss more. They did not know what my instructions were. They did not know what to do.

I was a bit shocked. I used actual sample theses. I usually had a discussion session. Most of all, I had listened to students' expectations in the first session and tried to accommodate them. But they were thinking about dropping the course. If so, above all, it was the teacher's responsibility. Maybe I talked about my experience too much. Maybe students already knew what I taught. 'Has any student talked to you about this?' 'No. No one told me. So I'm a bit surprised.' Yes, it would have been better if they had told me first and discussed the matters, which was part of the official procedure. But they directly sent complaints to the Faculty, and the Faculty contacted the Head of Department. Why did they not talk to me first? Was that because I was too difficult to approach? Was that because most of the students did not know me well? Was that because they did not trust me? It gave me a serious headache. I felt I was impeached; I thought I lost their trust. 'If they can't trust me, it's over. If I can't trust them, it's over . . . At least, I still should trust them.'

Back to my office, I looked into those complaints one by one. Some of them, I already explained several times during class. Others, I was actually planning to do from the upcoming presentation sessions. This led me to think about the difficulties and confusion surrounding communication itself. It took a lot of courage to stand in front of students in the next session. I tried to clarify things and apologised. In the following week, the first session of students' presentations began. I did not do anything new. I just did what I already planned before the complaints were filed—commenting on each student's thesis. At the end of that class, all students applauded me.

This particular event reminded me of what others had said about students before. 'You don't have to prepare much, because students don't study.' 'Don't believe students.' Whenever I heard such stories, I tried to ignore them; I thought I should still trust students. Distrust destroys everything, I said to myself. It however looked like I now almost came to agree with what I had heard. 'They might be right . . . ' I became very sad. I got hurt by what I tried to defend. And this brought back some sad memories—I had had a similar experience with other people. During the conversation with my friends, I defended a group of people who were being blamed. One of my close colleagues belonged to that group, and my initial experience was different from that of my friends. Some time later, the one I tried to defend would deeply hurt me by doing what my friends broadly described about the particular group in question. I was treated unfairly but could not say anything. Something hit me deep inside, something like a sense of betrayal. Whenever I recall that moment, my body still seems to shrink . . .

Back to my students. 'But of course, not always,' I quickly said to myself. And after all, it should be the teacher's responsibility to work things out. At least, teachers need to try. Yes, I need to keep trying. Why? Because distrust would destroy everything.

* * *

27 November 2015, YTN. It was two days before the anniversary of the case of KAL 858. The plane disappeared on 29 November 1987. I suspected that Hyunhee Kim would appear in the media this year as well. Unfortunately, I was right.

A programme of YTN (2015). 'How have you been?' asked the presenter. 'Well . . . now, the day after tomorrow is 29 November. That means it becomes the twenty-eighth anniversary of the case of the bombing of KAL. As such, many years have passed since then, but how could pain and sadness be healed and expressed all in words? They cannot be forgotten. So again, I'd like to take this opportunity to apologise to the victims and the families of the deceased . . . ' said Kim in a quiet voice with a remorseful look on her face. The same old stories were aired for about twenty minutes. 'Yeah . . . by the way, uhmm . . . May I?' said Kim. 'Yes, final words . . . ' answered the presenter. 'What I'd like to say is . . . well . . . in fact, in 2003 I was forced to leave during the Roh Moo-hyun administration, and up to now for about thirteen years, even now such a hard life . . . I have lived a refugee-like life,' said Kim in a complaining voice. 'The state has persecuted an individual like this . . . and framed me as a fake by distorting history—so although the state has committed such illegal criminal activities, it hasn't apologised at all and hasn't taken any responsibility either; it just keeps silent . . . ' said Kim in an aggressive tone.

I wondered how the families of KAL 858 would react. I would be reminded of Kim's interview when I returned to Korea. I stayed temporarily at a college in Seoul. There was a middle-aged man, who seemed to have a strongly hierarchical nature. He asked, or more precisely ordered me to do something that I did not have to. The reason was that I was much younger than him. I was offended, but not surprised. In Korea, heavily influenced by Confucianism, age is very often a significant factor in the code of social behaviour. At first I just did what he told me. It was unfair, but I accepted. Then similar things happened over and over again. And I decided to explain to him about the potential misunderstanding. He said that he thought I was a student working as an assistant. To him, I did not look like a visiting scholar with a PhD degree—I was regarded as a student assistant. Anyway, I thought that the problem had now been resolved. Unfortunately, he would later order me to do the same thing as if he did not care about my explanation at all. From his hierarchical point of view, I was still a student assistant.

This uneasy moment made me reflect on the rigid nature of hierarchy. The case of KAL 858 came to my mind. In the case of KAL, I would say that the government's official account has established itself as an absolute truth—it is at the top of the hierarchy. The families' stories and various unanswered questions offered different pictures, but they were overshadowed by Kim's

*narrative: the government has ignored or silenced them for many years.
Nothing else was more important than the official findings based on Kim's
contradictory statement. Because of this firmly maintained hierarchy of
accounts, other versions of the incident have been regarded as mere conspiracy theories or pro-North Korean remarks. Problems such as insufficient
evidence and the intelligence agency's manipulations do not count. Only the
top of the hierarchy matters. In a way, Kim's interview and my own experience taught me an important lesson: a strongly hierarchical nature within
narratives and power relations that make the hierarchy possible.*

* * *

This time I hope I will make it, I thought. I picked up the phone. I pushed the
button one by one.

'Hello. The National Archives of Korea. How can I help you?' 'Oh hello.
Uhmm . . . I am calling from abroad and there is one archive that I have been
trying to see for the last few years.' 'I see . . . Then you need to contact the
Reading Room. The number is . . . ' 'Sorry, but could you just transfer this
call to them? I am calling from abroad, so it's a bit . . . ' 'Ah . . . I understand.
But recently our phone system has changed and I'm afraid that you need to
call them directly. I am sorry sir.' 'Okay, then please tell me their number.'

A small problem from the start, but it was manageable. I hung up the phone
and made another call. 'Hello. The Reading Room at the National Archives.
How can I help you?' 'Hello. Well, I am calling from abroad and I'd like
to ask you about one particular archive.' 'Okay. What is it about?' 'Yes,
uhmm . . . This is about the case of KAL 858 or Hyunhee Kim. As far as I
know, the materials were transferred to the National Archives from the Truth
and Reconciliation Commission after the Commission was dissolved in 2010.
And in 2011, I visited the Archives to file a FOIA request. I mean, to see the
materials. But I was told that the transfer was still under way, so I was turned
away. Since then I have contacted again several times' 'Right . . . '

'Oh, by the way I am a researcher. And last time I was told that uhmm . . . If
I provide a document with a signature of the Head of Department's or my
manager's in it, then I would be able to see the materials. Just to make sure,
is this correct?' 'Yes, yes. So . . . you are a researcher from abroad.' 'Yeah,
I am a researcher at a foreign university. I am in Europe.' 'Okay . . . Then
could you wait a moment? Let me briefly check the materials. You said the
case of KAL 858, right?' 'Oh yes. Actually I have already located some of
the records on your website.' 'Right . . . Let me check.' 'Thank you, thanks
very much.' I felt good.

'Hello?' 'Yes, yes.' 'Yeah, so there are materials about the case.' 'Right,
thank you. Then again, just to make sure . . . So if I bring the signed document,

I would be able to see those materials. Is it correct? I am asking you this question again, because I am going to fly to Korea to see those materials.' 'Yes, if you provide us with the signed document, it would be okay.' 'And if I may, again to make sure, one more question please . . . I understand that the materials are named as closed records. But I can still file the request, and with the signed document from my institution, I would be able to see the materials. Am I correct?' 'Yeah . . . and there is the list of fees on our website. In case you make a photocopy or something, with that document, you will get a 50 per cent discount.' 'Alright . . . Thank you very much. Bye.'

I hung up the phone with delight. 'Yes, I think I can make it.' I then started preparing to leave for Korea—first of all, I talked to my Head of Department and got the signed document in a few days; I booked the cheapest flight ticket; I also made a reservation for the cheapest room at *goshiwon*, where students and low-income people temporarily stay to save money—it is a sort of mini apartment packed with a number of substantially small rooms. Once I arrive in Korea, it would be very hectic. So I tried to get things ready as much as I could. Most of all, I looked into the National Archives' website over and over again—I took notes about the already identified materials; I also read some relevant regulations of the National Archives. I became very focused.

Incheon International Airport, South Korea. I arrived in Korea with a cautious hope. It would be great if everything goes smoothly as planned, but sometimes things can happen. When I get back to the airport for a return flight, what would it be like? The following year would mark the thirtieth anniversary of the case of KAL 858. Think about it. Thirty years . . . Despite the official findings, there had been two reinvestigations. But the families and many other people are not quite sure what really happened in 1987. So it was absolutely important for me to see the materials at the National Archives. Even more so, because no one had yet tried to get these records. Obviously I wanted to make the most of this opportunity. Of course it was possible that the records would not reveal anything special. But still, it would be worth trying. 'Things will be okay. Yes, let's go.'

Three days later, still suffering from jet lag, I headed to the National Archives. From Seoul, it took almost two hours to get there—first by subway, by bus, then by walk . . . a long walk. I made the same trip with the same goal five years ago. Back then, things did not work. It was a very hot summer day. The sun was full of energy and shining all around me. It seemed to make fun of me. I hated that sunlight. I had to return feebly. Then what about this time? Well, we will see.

Right after I entered the Archives building, I had to pass through a small Security Check. 'Hello. Your bag please,' a guard said. Following the same guard, I then went to the reception. 'I'd like to go to the Reading Room please.' 'Can you tell me why?' 'There are some materials to look into.' 'Right. Your ID please. And fill out this form—your name, contact number and signature.' I handed in my passport. 'Don't you have a national ID card?' Yes, I had my card. But I did not want to show it, because there was my home address written on it. I tried to hide my personal information as much as I could. 'Well, I am a researcher working abroad, so . . . ' Without words, the guard nodded his head slantwise.

Looking at the form, now I nodded my head slantwise. 'Excuse me. I don't have a mobile phone.' 'Then, please write down your landline phone number.' 'Ah . . . There is no landline phone in my temporary accommodation.' 'So you don't have any contact number?' 'While I am here in Korea, I study in a library. There is a phone, but of course that's not mine . . . ' Yes, it was true. The guard stared at me suspiciously. 'Uhmm . . . I see. Then leave it blank.' I handed in the form. 'This is your visitor badge. Please return it when you leave.' 'Sure. Thank you.' It was a little bit tense, but not too bad.

The Reading Room on the first floor. 'Hello. Uhmm, I am a researcher at a foreign university. I have recently made a phone call, and I'd like to file a FOIA request.' 'Okay. Could you fill out a form? Over there, behind you please.' I picked up the form. It looked familiar, as I already checked it on the Internet—yes, I was prepared. 'Well, here it is.' 'Yeah. Please wait over there.' So far so good. While waiting, I looked around the place. There were several CCTV cameras. A few people came and went. It was relatively quiet. Then I could see several staff members talking to each other and shaking their heads.

'Mr. Sungju Park-Kang?' 'Yes.' 'I am in charge of this section of our unit,' a woman said with holding my application document in her hand. 'Well, I don't think you can see these materials . . . ' 'Sorry, what did you say?' 'Uhmm, these are all closed records and we can't show you them.' 'Yes, I know that they are currently closed records. That's why I came here to file the request. I already called this section from abroad and double checked.' 'Uh . . . I am not sure why you were told like that.' 'No, that's what I was told . . . it was . . . I don't know the name of the person I talked to, but it was a woman.' The section leader turned around to look at her colleagues. 'In this section, usually we have three people answering the phone. Me, the one who got your form and her.' The section leader pointed at another person, and asked. 'Have you recently got a call from abroad?' 'Yeah . . . ' her colleague blushed with confusion. 'Excuse me,' I intervened. 'So I called and you said, if I bring the signed document, I could file the request and would be able to see the materials.' ' . . . '

I felt that something was clearly wrong. 'Can you wait over there please?' said the section leader. Without a word I turned around and went back to where I was. The section leader and her team seemed to become very busy now. I sat and looked downwards. Ah . . . What should I do? I just sat there and did not move at all. My mind went almost blank . . . 'Mr Sungju Park-Kang?' It was the section leader's voice. I stood up and walked towards her. 'I am sorry, but I have to say this . . . I took a flight to come here because of these records. And before I flew, I made a call and brought the document as I was told. Then now, do I have to just go back? I am sorry, but I am really, very confused . . . ' I said straight away in an angry and sad tone.

'Yeah, yeah, I see. Calm down . . . I talked to my colleague who you had a conversation on the phone. According to her, she didn't exactly say what you described.' 'What? No, she . . . ' 'Yeah, yeah, wait a minute . . . That's what she told me. But anyway, I think there must have been some misunderstanding. Maybe we are partly responsible. So our suggestion is . . . As you said, you came here from far away—you can't just go back. So I suggest you fill out another form. Here it is—the application form for limited reading of closed records. Once you fill out this form, we will see what we can do.' I still wanted to protest against the phone conversation part. But I decided to restrain myself. 'Okay . . . Thank you. But still there is no guarantee that I can see the materials.' 'Well . . . First, please fill out this form. Once you return the form, we will see.'

I had no other choice. But at least they seemed to admit their fault in part and try to do something. I started filling out another application form. 'Well, here it is . . . ' The person I had a conversation on the phone received the application. It was a bit of an awkward moment. 'Thank you, and sorry but . . . Would it be possible to come back after lunch time? There is a dining hall on the top floor. It's not that expensive.' 'After lunch time? Ah . . . Yes,' I sighed slightly. Then I went to a toilet, and washed my face to get refreshed. Back to the Reading Room, I took a seat and decided to stay there for a moment before going to the top floor—I felt a bit exhausted.

'Mr Sungju Park-Kang? Hello, I work here. Can we have a word?' a man came and sat next to me. 'I just wanted to clarify things a little bit.' 'Ah . . . Yeah, go ahead,' I said quietly. 'Does your university have any associations with domestic schools here?' 'Well . . . I don't know.' 'I am asking you this, because according to our regulations foreign researchers are not allowed to see the materials here.' 'Excuse me?' 'Here's the thing. Foreigners who are working at Korean universities can see the records. Or foreign researchers who are affiliated with Korean schools here. In other words, to make it work for you, if you can get a document from any domestic schools that have connections with your university, I think you can see the materials.'

'Ah . . . Sorry. I am very confused. The regulations you mentioned—I haven't heard of such thing when I made the phone call before I came . . . ' 'Yeah, things are a bit complicated. Well, I think it may take some time for us to make a decision. So uhmm . . . You'd better go home today and we will probably contact you tomorrow.' 'Tomorrow? But I have just been told that I can come back after lunch time.' 'Our senior managers are busy at the moment, because there is an important conference going on today . . . I am sorry. So, can we call your number as you put in the application form?' I paused. I saw posters and flags about the conference, so that must be true. But still, what was going on here really?

'Uh . . . Excuse me, but I don't know what to say because I am so confused now. You have just mentioned something that I didn't hear when I made the phone call from abroad. And I was told to come back after lunch time, but you now say a different thing. I just don't know what to say . . . ' 'I am sorry . . . ' I sighed, and said. 'Okay, then I call it a day. By the way, I don't have a personal phone so I put some library's number in the form. It's not my number, so I might miss your call, but anyway that's my temporary contact number.' 'Yes, I see. Then goodbye for now,' bowed the man. 'Yeah . . . ' so did I.

On my way back, a two-hour journey felt almost like a two-day one. But at the same time, I got more motivated. I looked into the regulations of the National Archives and also the FOIA. The sections about 'foreign researchers' must be there somewhere. I already checked the regulations before coming to Korea but might have missed something about foreign researchers. I slightly regretted that I did not ask the staff member at the Archives to show the regulation in question. 'It's strange . . . ' I read the regulations over and over again but could not find anything that was mentioned at the Archives. The following morning at the library, I decided to go to the Archives again. I was supposed to wait until they contact me, but I wanted to take the initiative. There was a possibility that I could be just turned away like yesterday. But I chose to do something in a resolved manner. Yeah, let's go . . . I packed my bag to leave.

'Sungju? You have a call.' A librarian, an acquaintance of mine, said to me. 'Oh, to me . . . ? Do you know where this call is from?' 'It's the National Archives.' I was slightly alarmed. What are they going to say? . . . I cleared my throat, then picked up a receiver. 'Hello.' 'Hello. Mr Sungju Park-Kang?' 'Yes.' 'Ah, good morning. This is the section leader at the National Archives you met yesterday.' 'Ah, good morning.' 'We called yesterday as well, but couldn't speak to you. The thing is, we decided to let you see the materials.' 'Oh . . . that's . . . that's . . . Yeah, thank you very much.'

What a surprise. Indeed, what a relief! But I could not resist to go further. 'By the way, I was actually about to head to the Archives. Yesterday I was told that researchers working at foreign universities cannot see the materials at the National Archives. I have looked into your regulations several times but could not find anything like that. That means, you blocked me from exercising my legitimate right to get access information for no reason,' I said in a determined tone. 'Well . . . We didn't do it deliberately. Things are sometimes confusing. Anyway, so you are coming now?' I decided not to raise the issue anymore, as I was now allowed to see the files. 'Yes . . . I was about to leave.' 'Right . . . Then would you come a little bit later? Sometime in the afternoon? I have a meeting to attend soon.' 'Ah . . . Okay. Then I will see you in the afternoon. And thank you, thanks for your call.' 'Yes, see you soon. Bye.'

I hung up the phone. The librarian was staring at me, with a seemingly surprised look—my determined tone of protest must have struck the librarian. 'Oh, sorry . . . I . . . didn't expect to get this call,' I smiled shyly. A few hours later, I went to the National Archives. Something was in my hand—a beverage gift set. It was for the Archives, as a modest token of gratitude. I did not have to do it, I really did not. But I thought that a conciliatory gesture was needed. First, however, a short tense moment was waiting. There was the same guard at the reception as yesterday. He demanded a contact number. I repeated the same answer, and added. 'The Reading Room staff know that I am coming.' The guard stared at me less suspiciously than yesterday.

In the Reading Room the staff member, who talked to me on the phone before I came to Korea, greeted me. I gave her the gift set. 'Ah . . . No, you didn't have to do this.' 'No, no. Please take it. This is nothing much . . . By the way, yesterday I didn't have the chance to tell you this, because I was so confused, but uhmm . . . About you or any others here, personally I have no hard feelings. It was more like, you know . . . ' 'No, no problem. I understand. It's just good that you can see the materials.' 'Yeah, thank you.' Then the section leader came to me. 'Good afternoon.' 'Good afternoon. And thank you for letting me see the materials.' 'Yeah, because you came here from far away abroad, we decided to allow you to see them . . . So, the materials are ready now. You can sit there and read the records. You cannot take a picture or something, but you can make notes. Here's a pencil and paper . . . ' 'Oh, thank you.' 'And you may put your bag and belongings in a locker over there. Do you have any questions?' the section leader seemed to be very kind, unlike yesterday. 'Uhmm . . . Not at the moment. If I have, then I will ask you later.' 'Right . . . Then please take your time.' 'Yeah, thank you.' Wow, things are going smoothly now . . . I was glad.

The problem was how to review the materials within a limited time, effectively and carefully. Initially I thought that I could obtain copies of the materials, as I did before—from the US, the UK, Australia and Sweden. That way, I would be able to read and analyse the records whenever I want. This time however I could only see the materials at the National Archives—no copies other than the one here. Furthermore, I was scheduled to take a return flight in less than four weeks. Time management became vital.

Now, there were six volumes of records before me, roughly about 800 pages. I was not sure how to start; I just stared at the materials, which looked like a blue apartment miniature replica—with six floors and 800 households.

Then I decided to skim the whole floors first very quickly, to detect any-thing significant. I had already checked tables of contents of the materials on the website before I came to Korea. Using the list of priority sections I had already made would be a good idea. I nodded my head. Then I closed my eyes—I briefly prayed, not in a religious way though. I very often does this when I am about to do something important or very serious. It is my way of preparing things properly—with all my heart and soul. 'Alright, let's get started . . . ' I said to myself. Now, I entered this very special apartment. The first household on the ground floor: 'Knock, knock.' That was how my reading began.

In less than an hour I discovered some very sensitive and entirely new information, roughly five to six pieces. Interestingly enough, such examples included myself. An investigator at the TRC interviewed a former employee at the internal committee of the NIS; this employee was in charge of rein-vestigation of the case of KAL 858. The investigator was scheduled to go to the NIS to check and read the records there. The investigator at the Truth Commission wanted to get some advice and tips from him. One part of their conversation was about how to make the families of KAL trust the Truth Commission's result. 'Regardless of the Commission's findings, the families would not trust its result if the findings are not favourable to them. It would be better if you could persuade the families to recommend someone to join your team,' said the former NIS committee member (TRC 2008a: 60).

I paused. I could sense a sort of distrust between this former employee and the families of KAL. It was not so difficult for me to guess the reason. This person worked with the families to demand a formal reinvestigation before he joined the NIS committee; I met him as well. When the committee released their mid-term and final results, which concluded that the official findings by the South Korean authorities were correct in broad terms, the families did not accept them. And the families blamed this former activist who led the NIS committee's reinvestigation: 'He betrayed us . . . ' He might say that he did his best to find truth as *objectively* as possible. But the families, and many other people, did not think quite like that. So yes, there is a complicated story to consider.

It seemed that the Truth Commission investigator had contacted two people who were trusted by the families, but they did not want to get involved. The NIS committee member said, 'Why they didn't want to join the investigation—it seems suspicious' (Ibid.). And there, I was mentioned. Yes, I was approached by the investigator. I still remember that meeting. The investigator wanted to see me. We met at a small café. Before I entered the place, I had looked left, right and the surrounding area cautiously—you know, I was always aware of the potential surveillance by the NIS or the like. Once I entered the café, I looked at the inside carefully and took a seat.

The investigator asked me whether I would be interested in joining the TRC for their reinvestigation. That suggestion puzzled me. Most of all, when the Commission announced plans for recruitment of investigators, I applied for the job several times. But the Commission turned me down each time, which led me to decide to do my PhD project on the case. At the time of the meeting, I was scheduled to leave Korea in a few months. So both the timing and the Commission's intention seemed quite tricky and a little mysterious.

Another concern was that the investigator seemed to try to separate me from the families of KAL. 'The families are emotional and irrational. We need someone with whom it is possible to have a conversation.' The investigator may have said this to me as a compliment—to persuade me to join the team. If so, the investigator was mistaken. I was alarmed. Yes, the families *sometimes* could become emotional and irrational. But that was because they have been in pain for a long time. Their stories and behaviours needed to be understood in this context (and to me, the binary distinction between emotion and reason itself was problematic). Of course, this does not mean that what they say is always correct. But the families should not be neglected.

One other sensitive piece of information, from my point of view, was something about money. 'Judging from our experience, the families of KAL would be more interested in the matter of compensation than that of finding truth,' said the same former NIS committee member (Ibid.: 61). I paused. I thought that this remark could be the case for *some* families. Many families have had financial difficulties in the sense that most of the missing passengers were construction workers—the passengers and their families in general have humble backgrounds. And this committee member worked with the families much more closely than I did. Furthermore, the committee member actually reinvestigated the case. So it can be said that this person was in a better position to talk about such things.

But what I found from my research, from my interviews with about thirty-five families, tells a different story. Almost all the families did not prioritise the compensation issue. They still wanted to know what really happened; they still wanted to recover the seemingly dead bodies of their loved ones; they wanted to meet Hyunhee Kim to ask questions. That was why one family member did not close his eyes when he died. People tried to close his eyes after he had gone, but the eyes resisted being closed. He was buried with his eyes open in the end. There is an old Korean saying that one dies with open eyes if one has something deeply painful to solve at the time of death. This family member was very active in the reinvestigation campaigns—I myself could see this family on various occasions. So for me, it was difficult to agree with what the NIS committee member said: 'I think that the families are not interested in finding truth anymore' (Ibid.).

Also the efforts of the NIS to influence the Commission's reinvestigation seemed worth noting. The investigator interviewed the NIS agent, who appeared to act as a contact person. In case the Commission arranged an investigative interview with Hyunhee Kim, the NIS wanted the Commission to proceed in cooperation with the NIS. 'This is not an interference from us, but a cooperation,' said the NIS agent (TRC 2008b: 8). Actually, 'The NIS leadership was very interested in the direction of the investigation result.' In his interview report, the Commission investigator indicated that the NIS' cooperation would be needed in terms of *efficiency*. I was slightly alarmed.

The Truth Commission was supposed to conduct the reinvestigation as an independent government agency. And the reason why the families of KAL asked the Commission to reopen the case was that they could not trust the NIS' earlier reinvestigation process and its result. This problematic nature was acknowledged even by the Commission itself. Take the Commission's initial review report: 'Having analysed the NIS committee's mid-term report, it turned out that unanswered questions about the key issues still remain unanswered. [. . .] The materials produced by the ANSP [the current NIS] were just taken as evidence with no doubt' (TRC 2008c). Therefore, the NIS' seemingly kind suggestion needed to be assessed much more cautiously. Indeed, this is what the chairperson of the Commission thought as well: 'Do not consider the NIS' suggestion. Do the investigation fairly and accurately' (TRC 2008b: 8).

The most sensitive and entirely new piece of information was about Hyunhee Kim. The document showed very private and confidential information. I did not know what to do as I was almost shocked. I covered my mouth with both hands. A few quick thoughts came across my mind. First, I came to know something that was never known to the public. Secondly, this is very sensitive and private information—is it okay to see this? Thirdly, this sort of information usually should be blacked out—was the National Archives not aware of it? Lastly, with all this information—what to do next? I tried to think carefully.

Part of me said that I should forget this information because I was not supposed to see it. Part of me said that I needed to do something about it because I now knew. A difficult choice to be made . . . I closed my eyes, still putting hands over my mouth. For me, it seemed to be about ethical matters. Well, it would be okay for me to remember this information and use it for my research or something. After all, technically speaking, I did not do anything wrong or illegal—the Archives provided me with the materials upon my formal request. So I was just reading the records and sensitive information turned up, right there. But still, yes still . . . I did not feel comfortable. I kept thinking.

I opened my eyes. Yes, the decision was made. I quickly looked at the place where staff members were working. I then looked left, right and backwards pretending that I was doing a little neck exercise. There were CCTV cameras, but they seemed to be a bit far away from me. I moved a small piece of paper towards me, the summary list of tables of contents I brought which was already placed on the desk. I then made notes there slightly gulping—new and other private information. I folded this piece slowly and put it into my pocket quickly. I was not committing any crime, but it was nerve-wracking. Looking left and right, I stood up and walked towards the locker. I wanted to keep it in my bag there. I took out a key from another pocket. I opened the locker, then opened the bag and put the piece into it. Suddenly, however, I took out the piece and put it back into my pocket. My bag could be searched when I leave here, I thought. A meticulous measure was needed. I closed the locker and looked left and right again.

I then went outside the Reading Room. There was another CCTV camera. I walked towards a toilet, as if nothing was happening. Once I entered the toilet, confirming no one was there, I bent down my body. I put the piece of paper into my right sock. When I straightened up, there was a mirror—the only witness. I looked at the mirror—I was watching myself. I took a deep breath, kept looking at me. Nodding my head once, I left the toilet.

Since that day, small dramatic events continued from time to time. Most of all, by chance, I located more materials on the Archives' website—when I typed slightly different key words just out of curiosity, I could not believe it. A huge volume of records turned up . . . About 17,000 pages. Thanks to this remarkable but burdensome discovery, I had to spend almost all my time in Korea at the Reading Room. Actually, the amount was so huge that I could not read it all properly.

In the course of visiting this suddenly-built-gigantic-apartment, several unwanted guests wandered around me. Over the few weeks, several men came one by one and sat in front of me suspiciously. I may have over-imagined it but felt that I was being watched. Other than this, things went relatively smoothly. The guard kept asking for my phone number but gave up rather kindly; staff members at the Reading Room were kind and mostly cooperative; I had lunch, sometimes dinner as well, on the top floor of the Archives—the beautiful sky often comforted me. I was many times exhausted by the time of eating. On the last day at the Archives, I again bought a beverage gift set for staff members. They politely refused to take it though. I still felt that I had tried to do everything I could do. That was why I could go back to the airport and took a return flight with satisfaction.

Back to my office, I published a series of articles summarising my findings . . . except Kim's personal information—I did not plan to make this public from the beginning when I opened my eyes that (toilet) day. And I threw away that paper at the airport before I left Korea . . . On a side note, I personally felt sorry for Kim. After all, she is a human being. And she might be another victim of the ongoing war and divided situation on the Korean peninsula. Such a tragedy for Hyunhee Kim and all other Korean people—not to mention the missing passengers and their families. Then, who would be the winner?

* * *

26 November 2016, Seoul. About two million people held up candles across South Korea calling for President Park Geun-hye's resignation. Park was accused of letting her close friend manipulate state affairs. More fundamentally, she had been accused of incompetence as president and the destruction of democratic values since the start of her term. Her approval rating fell to a record-low of 4 percent amid ongoing protests over the last few weeks. It meant that the conservative Bulldozer *governments and their legacy since 2008, spanning the presidencies of Lee Myung-bak and Park Geun-hye, were in an unprecedented crisis. The largest protest since democratisation movements of the 1980s also brought a crisis to someone else . . . Hyunhee Kim. The situation was not favourable at all—the preferred political climate for Kim, which had allowed her to appear on television programmes and visit Japan as a VIP, fell into serious peril.*

Her life was changed in 1987. More than three decades on, she might not remember exactly how. One day, she found herself in South Korea. She was supposed to be on the other side, the North. She had learnt about the enemy land. That was part of her training, although she did not expect to be there, at least, not as a failed spy. It was the South Korean spy agency that made her life new again. They protected her, rather than tortured her. She got a job, not a death sentence. People wondered. Yes, they did. In South Korea during the 1980s, when a military general was the president, many innocent people were tortured and passed off as a spy. That was what sustained the military regime in the name of security—'Look, North Korean spies infiltrated. The North is our main enemy. They are not humans. And national security must come first.' But when Kim the real North Korean spy, according to the official investigation, came, she was treated rather gently. This might have made even Kim puzzled, I suppose.

There were a number of fabricated spy cases in which she was involved indirectly. One special case was brought out in April 2013. A woman made a false confession about her brother after the South Korean spy agency abused and persuaded her. This woman's false confession turned a Chinese-Korean, who had defected from North Korea and made a new start at Seoul's local government, into a North Korean spy. This sort of manipulation was nothing new. Still, many people were surprised to hear what the agency told this frightened Chinese-Korean woman: 'If you make a false statement (that your brother is a spy), like Hyunhee Kim's case, in return, as the government, we can guarantee your safety and new life here in the South' (Lee 2013). The exhausted woman, isolated and sometimes hit by interrogators over a period of six months, finally said yes. So, another invention of a spy. Should Kim be happy about her sacred part in this marvellous creation?

The spy agency arranged numerous media interviews for Kim. It seems that she mostly repeated the same script instructed by the agency: I was used by North Korea. *The agency also arranged various lectures on national security. Kim repeated the story that she was given to deliver:* North Korea is our enemy. *In addition, she became a best-selling writer at some point. The agency hired someone as a ghost-writer. The book was published under Kim's name:* I want to be a woman *(not a terrorist). Did she want all of these? I wonder.*

* * *

The TRC reinvestigated the case of KAL 858, but its attempt ended with no official result. That was because the family members withdrew their request to investigate. Once the Commission was dissolved, civil society as a whole began a legislative campaign to launch a second-term Commission. Their hope has been that the new agency, with more powers and resources, would dig into various cases that have not been investigated thoroughly enough.

I have been greatly interested in the issue of the Commission not only because the agency could reinvestigate the case, but also because it pursues transitional justice in general. Indeed, in the course of the initial establishment of the Commission in 2005, I actively worked with other people to pass a law. Then I left for Europe and have been away from Korea for many years now. I could not actually contribute to the second legislative campaign, which made me feel a bit guilty. It was therefore no wonder that I was more than determined to do as much as I could during my stay in Korea.

This determination led me to see Kyungho Ahn, who worked for the Commission as a chief investigator. We first met when we worked together as civil society members to establish the Commission in 2004–2005. He asked me to come to the National Assembly; he was busy there to engage in the legislative process. We were supposed to meet at one of the entrances of a building where lawmakers' offices are located. I used to come to this building and knew where the entrance was. So I was waiting there, but for some reason he did not turn up. As I did not have a mobile phone, I just kept waiting. He finally showed up and said that the building's structure had changed due to a renovation, meaning I was at the wrong place. Yes, while I was in Europe, a lot had changed indeed. But the issue of transitional justice, pain of the victims of state violence and their families remained unchanged, I thought. Anyway we had lunch together. 'I suppose you have missed Korean food.' Apart from our main dish, he ordered a popular Korean snack called *tteokbokki* (stir-fried rice cake) for me. It is quite spicy, and I do not like such food. I tried to eat the spicy food happily though, partly because I wanted to respect his way of caring for me and partly because I had felt guilty while I was away, as mentioned.

Another thing I did was to join a protest organised by the National Association of Bereaved Families of Civilian Victims in the Korean War. To my best knowledge, this organisation was one of the most active civil society groups that was campaigning for the second-term Commission. They had been holding the so-called one-person demonstration in front of the National Assembly. Usually on weekdays during the parliamentary sessions, several members in turn stood with a placard for about an hour each, one by one. At the time of my visit, the protest was around the 350th. It was quite a cold winter. I checked the time and place of the protest on their website and went there.

On my way, I thought about how to introduce myself, how they would react to my visit, what I would do while standing there and so on. Upon my arrival, however, I could not see anyone there. It was early in the morning, so I just waited. Still, no one turned up, and it was snowing so I decided to call the person in charge. The problem was that I had to find a public phone booth, because I did not have a personal phone. I thus had to go back some distance. 'Oh, the time is actually changed. Someone will be there. Sorry.' 'No problem!' Indeed, that was totally okay for me. Such waiting was really nothing, compared to the long period of about sixty years that the families had had to endure so far.

People arrived later. They were families and relatives of the victims massacred during the Korean War. They seemed to be surprised by my visit. I asked them to let me stand first. There was a placard with numbers and words on it. The number '350' meant that the protest marked its 350th time. The phrase 'Investigate Civilian Massacres!!! Pass the Special Law!!!' referred to the demand for the establishment of the TRC. I finally started my protest. Various thoughts came and went. Most of all, I was glad that I had this opportunity to do my little part in the legislative process. I embraced the moment to pay off my debt, and sense of guilt. I was grateful that I had managed to do something very actual and tangible.

It was cold and snowing. I looked up the sky. White, thin snow was falling. I stayed focused on snow for a while. Thin, and white. It was similar to something . . . It looked like bone ash. Yes, ashes of the victims killed in the war. It seemed to me that snow-like bone ash was falling. Numerous people had been massacred, and in many cases the burial places are not known exactly. A lot of bodies of innocent people are still somewhere in the ground. To recover those remains, to know what really happened, and to seek justice, the Commission needed to be launched again as soon as possible. But that was not the case. So sad, so tragic that even the sky was weeping. Hence tears, or snow and bone ash were falling . . . That was what I thought.

Since my first protest in solidarity with the victims' families, I had continued to turn up for about one and a half months. I was usually the first person to arrive and start the protest of a day. A placard was placed in a storage-like space around the entrance. I would go to this storage to pick up the placard. There was a small toilet around the entrance as well. It was not visible enough, so many people did not seem to realise that the toilet was there. Once our own turn ended, we protesters went to this toilet to warm ourselves— there was a heater inside. Both the storage and toilet belonged to the National Assembly. Although I was not happy with the parliament that had not passed the law, I was grateful that we could use its facilities.

The more complicated feeling was yet to come. It was another morning in front of the National Assembly. I finished my share of the protest and stood next to a family member on duty. Suddenly several guards from the National Assembly started to surround the entrance. Something must be happening, I thought. Then I could see a black car coming. That car had a rather different licence plate, meaning someone in a car was not an ordinary person. The car came closer to the protest site and the family member bowed deeply before the car. Yes, it was a very deep and big bow, which made me a bit surprised. He said that the passenger in the car was the Speaker of the National Assembly, a very special figure indeed. The Speaker hopefully understood why the family members were protesting there.

Apart from that, seeing the victim's family bowing like this deeply saddened me. He had not done anything wrong, but to me, he bowed as if he were apologising to the Speaker. Politicians like the Speaker should have apologised to the families of victims for not having been able to work out the issue of the massacres. It was not fair. But I could also see why he did that. The families like him did not have much choice. Whether it was protesting or bowing, he was just doing his best on that cold morning. The family member's deep bow seemed to symbolise a sense of desperation. In retrospect, the bow also represented his determination to continue the fight.

The parliamentary session ended in late December, but the families could not just stop the legislative campaign. Indeed, the aforementioned deep bow was a symbol of their determination as well. They now decided to stage a protest around the Blue House or Office of the President. The Moon Jae-in government announced its one hundred core policy tasks and the establishment of the second-term TRC was among them. According to the plan, the legislative process should have been finalised by the end of 2017, and the Commission would have to be launched by the first half of 2018. At the beginning of the new year, it was clear that the government's plan was not fulfilled. Of course, it was not entirely the government's fault; the parliament was mainly responsible for the delay. Still, President Moon and his government were not free from blame. That was why the families wanted to continue the protest in front of the Office of the President, while the parliament was not in session. It was 1 January 2018, the very first day of a new year. We gathered at Fountain Plaza, a public square in front of the Office. To my surprise, there were also other groups of people who had been protesting for various purposes. I was surprised not because they came to protest, but because they came on the first day of the year. There were many people who felt so desperate that they could not stop their demonstrations even on 1 January, whatever the reason.

We began our one-person protest for a certain period of time one by one, as we had done earlier. Then, security guards working for the Office approached us. I was alarmed. It turned out that they just wanted to know why we had come. Furthermore, as we were newly arrived protesters, they told us about some rules and safety measures. They were relatively kind. I say this, because South Korea had just gone through quite violent and chaotic times during the previous two conservative governments. It was an established view that democratic values and human rights were generally degraded during Lee Myung-bak and Park Geun-hye's presidencies. Many legitimate demonstrations and critical voices against the government were largely unwelcomed. Police and security guards did not have good reputations then.

But now I could feel that the atmosphere had clearly changed. A few days later this change would be reconfirmed in an unexpected manner. Guards brought us hot packs or hand warmers. They knew that it was not easy to hold protests in the cold winter. They also gave us warm beverages. More than that, they distributed this winter-protest-survival kit to other protesters as well. This was probably one of the warmest surprises I had ever had.

For this protest in a new place, a banner was used along with a placard. We wore a placard around our necks, then held the banner. The word on the banner *kyokjaeng* means that a person suffering from resentment is appealing to the king by hitting a gong, a musical instrument. It was a Korean tradition practised by ordinary people some hundreds of years ago, during the Chosun dynasty. We did not have an actual gong, but I hoped that our desperate wish, running through the winter wind, could reach the President's ears.

Holding the banner was not easy though. It was a rather big object of almost 2 m. This big banner was attached to a long stick. Against the wind, you would need to have some skills to maintain your balance while standing. These skills were indeed necessary, because we began to hold one more banner, a bigger one, from the following week onwards, so we were equipped with one placard and two banners. What made things more complicated was the weather. Usually the coldest month in South Korea is January. The year of 2018 was no exception. I wore gloves, but they were not warm enough to protect my hands from the cold winter. Also I wore two pairs of socks, but they were not enough either. Once I had finished my share of duties, I had to stay right next to a heater in my accommodation to warm fingers and toes. Back then, I thought that it was too much—holding three objects and standing for an hour in the very cold winter. Furthermore, its effectiveness was in doubt—not many people, let alone President, stopped by and read the words on the placard or banners. My thoughts still remain the same. The question is then why families did so. Based on the circumstances at the time and my observations, one possible answer would be that they were desperate. As mentioned before, the families just did everything they could. The cold winter did not matter much.

Just like in the earlier protest in front of the National Assembly, I was usually the first one who started the day's protests. The storage of protest equipment was arranged in cooperation with another protest group situated near the Office of the President. They were labour union members who worked in the technology sector. Their company was owned by a foreign business and the management had laid off many workers. For the workers' perspective layoffs were illegitimate. They wanted their jobs back. President Moon met them when he was the opposition leader in 2015 and promised that he would try to work out the problem. The issue however was still unresolved, so they decided to stage a protest near the Office where Moon resided. They had started the protest in a tent in November 2017, and kindly agreed to take care of our placard and banners. Upon my arrival at the place, I headed to the tent to collect the things. Thanks to their help, the protest arrangement went smoothly on a daily basis.

During our protest, we could hear the so-called protest song coming from their tent. They turned up the music loud to cheer themselves up. That song also cheered me up. I really liked it so I tried to memorise lyrics and later identified the title of the song: 'Breaking this ice-like world.' It sounded like a perfect song in the cold winter and in this mean world.

We could not see President Moon around the protest site, but we did see the President of the National Association of Bereaved Families of Civilian Victims in the Korean War. He visited us to cheer us up. And he gave me a surprise present. It was a cake. He and other members seemed to be grateful to me, a stranger and relatively young person, for joining their protest. I was moved by the cake that the president brought me. The problem was that I did not like sweets. He looked a bit disappointed, but I sincerely thanked him. Although I did not take it, this surprise cake present demonstrated that I had gained trust from the families. Being trusted by others, that is a wonderful thing. I was happy.

Actually, I had met the president several days after I initially joined the protest around the National Assembly. A coordinator of the protest conveyed his message to me that he wanted to see me in person. I was a bit surprised. It appeared that he was impressed by my continuous participation. I was told that he was recovering from major surgery. That was why he could not join the protest himself. So I agreed to see him. The meeting took place at a small café in his residential area. Like many other members, he was elderly. The president was a very knowledgeable person. He said that some families of the victims are mainly interested in compensation rather than truth. The coordinator added that several members of civil society did not like the president because of this critical opinion. I felt that there were some long and complicated stories. Anyway, it was good to see him again.

I would later get to know more about a conflict among the families indicated by the president. When I read some materials, I realised that the name of this family organisation was written differently. It was strange. So I checked the organisation's website again and realised that there are two groups with similar names: the Association of Bereaved Families of Civilian Victims and the Association of Bereaved Families of the Civilians Massacred. In addition to the similar names, they both used exactly the same logo on their websites; I was aware that there were two different sites, but just assumed that they were connected to each other.

The aforementioned president actually belonged to the Civilian Massacred group, not the Civilian Victims group as I initially thought. I was quite confused. It turned out that some members were split from the Civilian Victims organisation, then set up their own group, which became the Civilian Massacred organisation. There must have been serious disagreements among the members of the original group, which led to the break-up of the organisation around 2015. I guessed that the disagreements might be concerned with the issue of compensation, as briefly mentioned by the aforementioned president. I could not know the exact circumstances and still do not know either. It was very sad that these families were going through internal confrontations. The victims were killed by the Korean conflict and their families were distressed by the organisation's internal conflict. How sad it was.

There was another thing that raised an uncomfortable question. At some point during the protest, confusion emerged over exactly how long we had staged protests. We changed number cards on the placard on a daily basis to mark how many days we had stood. That day, for some reason, we could not find a suitable number card for the last digit. Then one family member suggested that we just put another available card, which had a higher number. Using this improvised number card meant that we appeared to have been protesting for longer than we actually had, which was not true. Another member pointed out the problem saying that the number was wrong. But the proposer answered that, after all, except for us nobody would actually care about this; people even did not know that we were protesting there. So, the families decided to put the wrong and higher number card on the placard.

Although it felt wrong, I just kept quiet because I was not a family member. It was an awkward moment. Related to this, the starting time for the daily protest was marked wrongly on the website's briefing section. It said that the protest started at 7 a.m., but the actual starting time was 8 a.m. Maybe the protest initially did start at 7, then the time changed later because of the cold weather. The thing was that this change was not reflected in daily briefings afterwards, giving the impression that again, we protested longer than we actually did. It was a minor thing, but it still did not feel right.

I would get more confused when I came back to Europe. By then I had already wrapped up my protest and fieldwork but kept visiting the organisation's website. There, one family member left a comment on the group's press conference in May 2018. 'While the media have been reporting tediously again and again on trivial issues such as #MeToo, they covered our event just once.' The words 'trivial . . . #MeToo' sounded problematic. As a researcher in the community of feminist IR, I know and believe that the #MeToo movement is a serious matter. Having read the family member's comment, confusion and uneasiness engulfed me. I supported the families and joined their protest, and now saw such a comment. Of course, it was just one member's note, so I did not want to rush to generalisation (although there could have been many more members who shared that view). Also, given the families' frustrating circumstances, I could understand why this comment was posted.

This issue and the above uncomfortable questions made me think about ethical dilemmas regarding fieldwork. When you find the informant's words and actions ethically problematic, what can you do? When you and the informant have seriously different views, what can be done? More fundamentally, who does decide a certain thing is problematic and how? I do not think that there are any correct and easy answers. But at least, one might need to acknowledge that human affairs are complicated and the world is not black and white.

Going back to the protest near the Office of the President, I was able to participate until the end of January. Time just seemed to fly. The last day came. As usual, I collected the placard and banners at the labour union's tent and started my protest. I briefly looked back on the last one and a half months. The sense of indebtedness made me join the families in protesting. I felt that I had now paid off some portion, yes only some portion of debt. I wished to participate until the very end of the legislative process. But there were other plans and commitments that I had to deal with, especially back in Europe. It was time to say goodbye. I thanked the families for letting me join, and the families thanked me for being with them. The coordinator said, 'You burst on to the scene like a comet, and did a lot.' But the pleasure was mine. So the coordinator was given something unexpected by me, like I was given the surprise cake by the families. It was a small donation. The coordinator refused to accept the money and tried to return it to me. I ran away very fast. When enough distance was secured, I turned back and waved my hands.

Entanglement

'As long as he fails to let loose of KAL 858, I would caution for a "one-trick pony." Although he has all the trappings of a good scholar, as long as he does not branch out into new territory, I wonder whether he can really qualify to become a docent,' the statement read. I had applied to become a docent and my works were evaluated by two assessors. The first reviewer's statement was positive, but the second one was not. Consequently, and unexpectedly, my docentship could not be approved.

I was heartbroken. I tried to respect and acknowledge the professional assessment of that expert. But frankly speaking, it was not easy to accept what the assessor described. I explored my case study in terms of IR, Korean studies, gender studies, narrative studies and the issue of transitional justice, from an interdisciplinary perspective—situating my work within a bigger picture. All my effort, however, was dismissed as the 'one-trick pony' project. Maybe my effort was not sufficient. Maybe I was not capable enough to do this job. Or maybe, this evaluator was simply right—I should forget KAL 858 and move on, hunting for a new case study or something more important than the KAL case. To be fair, I myself was aware of the risk of digging into one case, regardless of the various approaches I took. Seeing the statement, I felt deeply hurt. 'Well, let's not take this personally. Good medicine tastes bitter . . . Yeah, it could be something like that.' Then has the time finally come for me to stop? The time to let go of KAL 858?

There is one experience that I would never forget. The families of KAL 858 had held a protest in front of the Memorial Tower in the summer. This monument was built in memory of those missing passengers, but in accordance with the official findings by the government. The families rejected the government's findings and wanted to reopen the case. They thus decided to have a performance—destroying part of the Tower, not physically but symbolically. They wanted to send a strong message, because the government had not listened to them; the government kept ignoring the families' voice. When the day came, there was a heavy police presence. In spite of the high tension, the families, human rights activists and I proceeded to do the performance.

We picked up rubber hammers. Almost immediately it became chaos. The police interrupted and tried to confiscate all the materials prepared for the ceremony. The families and I resisted as much as we could. The police then began to scatter the crowd by force. Some families screamed and cried. The police separated each protester from the crowd one by one—four police officers grabbed all the arms and legs of protesters, and the protesters were literally lifted up by the police, then dragged from the performance site. I was no exception. While I was being dragged, I tried to escape and shouted something. It was an ugly scene.

But the protesters did not just give up. Shortly after, several people gathered again at a place not far away from the performance site—they gathered in the middle of a road, around a pedestrian crossing. They sat here and there, and waged a sit-in protest: some holding a big banner, some holding a small placard and some even lying on the ground. I quickly joined them. The police began to approach again. An old lady next to me still had the rubber hammer. This woman was protecting the hammer—she sat, both hands clutching it tightly. As the police approached further, I held this family member's hands, thereby forming more of a shield for the hammer. This rubber hammer might have meant nothing to others—it was just a little toy. But to the families of KAL 858, and to me, it was a hammer of conscience and determination. Strictly speaking, the planned performance had been blocked by the police, so the hammer was no longer useful. But at that moment, to that old woman and me, it meant everything. The meaning survived the usefulness, effectiveness and scientific calculation . . .

And please remember, it was a summer's day. We sat on the hot asphalt pavement—sweat and tears were mixed. That day, I saw each family, and myself, shouting and crying. I saw the desperation, anger and resilience. This experience left a deep trace on my mind. To me, the case of KAL 858 was not a *single case*, in which 115 people disappeared—there were more than *115 cases*, in which each passenger, and each family, had been destroyed.

I have been told many times that I should not focus on a single case study for too long. While I agreed with the point, I have begun to reconsider the concept itself. If a 'single case study' means a study on the same case from the same perspective, then it could constitute a problem. But my approach, I believe, was not like that. I first dealt with the case from a traditional social science perspective. I then consulted, for instance, feminist IR and narrative studies. The case has been reinvestigated by truth commission-like bodies, so this is also about the issue of transitional justice. There are many ways to work on the case. This is not unique to KAL 858. The same single case can be approached from different perspectives.

More broadly, I would say that the term single case contains an assumption that events, humans and all different kinds of being can be completely separated from each other. But is it possible that every human, social and natural affair can exist purely on its own? I am not brave enough to say yes.

In that sense, there is no such thing as a single case study, if I may say so. Let's also take a brief moment to remember 115 individuals who were on board the plane. Can all those people's lives be compressed and squeezed into one single box? What about their families? And what about others who might have been affected by the case in different ways? Can we really line up all these people, turn them into one baton and call them a single case?

Fortunately, my docentship was later approved—the reviewer in question did not follow instructions given by the administration and therefore the statement was declared invalid; subsequently additional actions were taken, which led to the positive result. Nonetheless, the reviewer's words hurt me. In academic and scientific terms, the reviewer might be right. 'I wish the ring had never come to me. I wish none of this had happened.' Frodo said in the film *The Lord of the Rings*. Likewise, I said to myself. 'I wish KAL 858 had never come to me. I wish I had never written the thesis. I wish none of this had happened.' Indeed, there have been many moments when I wondered why I was devoted to this case, to this Cold War mystery. I thought and thought again. But I could not come up with an answer. Perhaps I knew something in the early days, and gradually forgot? Maybe, maybe not. The case of KAL 858 is a mystery, and the reason why I keep pushing myself becomes another mystery.

At the end of the day, life is not mathematics. Part of it can be mathematics, but our life as a whole cannot be about logic and numbers. Life is full of questions that cannot be explained—or do not need to be. You just have to live through it. Eventually you may find an answer, and maybe not. But everything you try, everything you hope, will be connected in the end in one way or another, often in a miraculous way. They will become part of something. You become life, life becomes you. So if someone asks me why I am so interested in this case, I would probably say, 'Well, I don't know . . . That's just me. That's Sungju.'

I know a thing or two about what it is to lose someone close, without warning. I was eighteen when my father passed away. At that very moment, I was away to take a college entrance exam in another city. My father was away too—he worked for the provincial government and was dispatched to cover one of the local areas for a number of years at that time. It was January, the coldest month in Korea. I was with my classmates and teachers preparing for the entrance exam, which would take place in a few days. Then I was called to a separate place by one of the teachers. 'Something happened to your father. Return as soon as possible.' The teacher did not say that much. Several things were already arranged. A flight ticket, not a train nor a bus, was booked for me and my relative was waiting for me at the airport.

Obviously I was anxious, but did not want to worry too much. There was still some time before I headed to the airport. I decided to finish a self-test mock exam that I was doing right before I was called. Maybe I needed some distractions, not to think too seriously about my father. The score? Forty-four out of one hundred. I was alarmed, deeply. Not because of the unexpectedly low mark though—what struck me, what troubled me was the number four. In Korea and other East Asian countries, this number symbolises death . . . I tried to remain calm.

At the airport, my relative did not tell me much about my father's condition. While waiting for the flight, I wanted to check the situation by myself. I walked around and found a public phone. I called my father's office. I cannot remember exactly why I did that. Probably I called my home, but could not reach my mother. 'Hello. May I speak to Mr Park please?' 'Excuse me, but who is this calling?' 'This is his son.' A brief silence followed. 'Well . . . I thought you were already informed . . . He passed away. I am sorry . . . ' I was left speechless. Big tears, heavy as crystal marbles, spoke only. I was just standing like that for a few minutes. It turned out that no one, my teacher or relative, had dared to deliver the news to me. Most likely, my mother might have asked them not to tell the news, because she did not want to upset me too much. Or she might have wanted to tell me directly. But it did not matter anymore. I had found out by myself.

What did I think about on my way? I cannot remember much. There is one thing that I clearly remember though. That was my first time flying. And there are always some mysterious elements in any first time experience in our lives. My first flight was no exception. The plane was flying high, yet my world was flying as low as possible. The plane was flying fast, yet my world was flying as slow as possible.

The hospital funeral hall was quiet. It was located on the basement floor, where several open places were to be used. I looked around the place. My father was not there yet. Probably one place was occupied at that time. A photo of the deceased and an incense burner assured me that this was not a joyful place. I went outside to wait. I looked at the sky. Various thoughts came and went. Then a car came, the hospital vehicle. Its door was slowly opened. My mother was there. I stepped into the car. My mother hugged me and cried. 'I am okay. To me, you are enough. I am okay, as long as there is you . . . ' My father's body was in a coffin. Later my brother arrived. Now in the basement funeral hall, all the family gathered. I, along with my brother, knelt down in front of my father's photo. My mother greeted mourners.

My father had passed away suddenly. It was a heart attack caused by high blood pressure. I did not have the chance to say goodbye, neither did my father. He had just gone. That was it, just like that. In the blink of an eye, you may lose someone. In the blink of an eye, this someone would not leave you though. Rather, this someone would *live* in you. This someone would still be with you, for a while if not forever. Probably, yes, probably because it is totally unexpected—too sudden to be real. It may take some time for you to take in. More like Newton's first law of motion, there is the law of inertia in loss.

This is where the case of KAL 858 comes in. Someone just disappeared— not one or two, but 115 people. And their families were waiting for them, right there in the airport. They were about to reunite. They were about to hug. But what happened? There was no chance to welcome them back, not to mention no chance to say goodbye. I myself had such an experience. Perhaps that is why I seem to devote myself to work on this case. It is the suffering that connects me to those families. I am no stranger to the sudden loss. I know what it is . . . Well, at least partly. Yes, only partly. The shock and pain of the families of KAL should be far more different. I was sure about my father's death, while those families could not. I saw my father's body, while those families could not. I knew the cause of death, while those families could not. It would be hard for me to know exactly what their lives were like. What I do know is that they needed someone to listen. And I have been trying to listen . . .

By the way, there is one delicate thing in my case. I did not attend my father's funeral, I missed it. More precisely, I chose to miss it. On the day of the funeral, I went back to my classmates and teachers—I took the college entrance exam. My father always wanted me to go to the best university in the country. And this university's entrance exam coincided with the funeral. 'Dad, what would you want me to do?' I asked. The answer was not so difficult. Following that answer, however, came at a price. That I did not attend the funeral has since become a lifelong burden to me.

'You will get the key to the problem through attentive listening.' I often say to myself . . . There was a farewell gathering before I left Korea to do my PhD on the case of KAL 858. The families of KAL organised the gathering. I did not like their idea. I wanted to leave quietly. I did not want the families to spend time and money in arranging the meeting. Maybe the families could not just let me go like that. I myself was not sure when I would return. So I very reluctantly agreed with the suggestion. I would soon however regret it. The families booked a place at a hotel. It was too much for me. 'At a hotel . . . ? This is not right.' I could not accept it. But I did not have much choice. The families had already invited people and things were set. In the end, I went there with a heavy heart. The families also prepared a present for me. The gathering itself was already too much for me, so I tried not to accept it. 'It is not polite to turn down our gift,' the families said and smiled. I reluctantly opened it. It was a luxurious pen and propelling pencil. The families seemed to want me to work hard with this pen and pencil. But again, they were too much. 'If I may, please let me take the pencil only. Someday, when this case and everything will have been settled, let me take that pen as well.'

But there was one thing that I gladly accepted—a fortune cookie, which was served after dinner. 'Open it!' 'Yes, this can be really interesting.' With a curious and innocent look on my face, I opened the cookie slowly . . . 'You will get the key to the problem through attentive listening.'

Except for that fortune cookie and pencil, I have always tried not to accept anything from the families of KAL. After a meeting, forum or press conference we often had lunch or dinner together. And I wanted to pay my own bill. But the families always stopped me. 'What are you doing? No, we can't let you do that.' It was a somewhat tricky moment for me. But I had my own strict rule, and had been trying to keep the rule as much as I could. Then how did I pay my own bill? I made a donation to the families' organisation.

I still remember my first donation. It was when I had published a journal article on the case. I was commissioned to write this article and got paid. The thing was that I did not feel comfortable—it seemed like I made profits at the expense of the families' suffering. So I donated all this money. The families of course did not want to take it. 'No, no, no, no! Please don't do this!' 'Please take it, please . . . You know, I have wanted to do this for several years. Do you remember my unification thesis case? There was prize money. And I planned to donate part of that money. But as you know, the award was cancelled, so was my plan . . . Please take it. I have long wanted this to happen. Please, I mean it . . . I insist.' Only then the families hesitantly accepted the donation. Speaking of profits, when I published a book based on my PhD thesis, I donated a royalty as well.

For the families' part, they always wanted to give me something. When I briefly got back to Korea for fieldwork and attended a memorial ceremony on the anniversary of the case, the families seemed to come up with a plan. After the ceremony, one family said to me. 'Thank you very much for coming from so far away.' 'Please, no worries . . . It's good to be here.' 'When do you leave again?' 'Well, in two days.' 'Oh, so soon . . . ' 'Yes, indeed.' 'Then, can I hold your hand? I mean, you are leaving soon again, so . . . ' 'Hahaha . . . Okay, sure. Yes.' The family grabbed my hand. 'Um . . . ah . . . ' I felt strange. There was something on my hand—money in an envelope! Well, what did I do? I stepped back. 'I am so sorry!' I shouted. I then threw the envelope on the ground gently and ran away like Usain Bolt, a 100 m sprinter. Then from a distance . . . I bowed, and smiled.

Over the years while I was working on the case of KAL during and after my MA project, the president of the family association of KAL came to trust me highly. I was told that the president even cried when I left Korea to do my PhD project. It was this same president who organised the farewell gathering for me and also tried to give me the money in the envelope later. Although I had left Korea, I often called the president to say hello. The president always welcomed my call and enjoyed the conversation. It seemed that the president really, and seriously valued me. Of course I was grateful. But I also felt sorry. The president was far older than me. And sometimes she seemed to value me too much or trust me excessively, which I did not think I deserved. Whenever the president highly praised me or told me something far more than I deserved, I thought: it is sad that such a senior like the president tries to make someone very young like me proud . . . Indeed, particularly in Korea where the Confucian hierarchical order is still largely cherished, such a relationship between a senior and a younger person is quite rare.

For me, there was another thing to be cautious about: the researcher-researched relationship. I did not want the president to think that I called her just because I was working on the case of KAL—to get information about the case. As a person, not as the researcher or interviewer, I respected the president. So for example, when a conversation ended, I almost always waited until the president hung up first. Somehow I felt that I should wait—getting off the phone first right after the conversation might give her an unintended impression: 'Let me go now, because I got what I wanted.'

Most importantly, I did not want to place a burden on the president or any other families. When I arranged an interview with the president, I deliberately chose to visit her home outside meal times. It was when I briefly got back to Korea. There was a reason. When I first interviewed her some years ago, the president suggested that I visit the house around dinner time. I asked her to change the time, because I knew that the president wanted to prepare a meal for me. But the president so strongly insisted that I just agreed. Once I got there: surprise, surprise. It was like I came to a luxurious buffet restaurant. I was so sorry . . . although the president did not think like that at all.

This time I have to be very clear, I thought. I managed to persuade the president to meet at 2 p.m.—I made up an excuse. 'I have an extremely significant appointment around 4.' A white lie, if you like. So yes, after lunch and before dinner time. 'Now, she can't prepare any meal for me . . . Hahaha.' When I arrived at the president's house, I was warmly and very kindly welcomed. 'Tick, tock, tick, tock . . . ' It was almost 3:30 p.m. I was cautious. 'Thank you so much for today. I am sorry, but as I said . . . I'm afraid that I need to leave now for another appointment.' 'Oh, so soon? It went fast . . . ' 'Yeah . . . Anyway, thank you very much. Then, let me . . . ' I stood up.

'No, no! Wait, wait!' the president shouted while rushing into the kitchen, like Usain Bolt. 'No, no! Please. I really have to go now. Sorry, but . . . ' 'No, you can't do that. Please wait.' 'No . . . I have to leave right now. I mean

it.' 'Just a second . . . I have something for you here . . . ' 'Ah . . . I will
be late. Really . . . You don't have to do anything . . . ' 'Wait, wait . . . It's
almost done . . . ' 'Ah . . . Please don't. Really . . . ' 'Please wait. Just a minute . . . ' 'But . . . ' Then I stopped protesting. You may wonder why. That was
because . . . the president's hands were shaking. She was desperately trying to
pack food so quickly that her hands were trembling. Looking at those shaky
hands, with an immensely heavy heart, I could not say anything. I was just
standing there, with tearful eyes.

I faced one of the most challenging moments of my research and life when a
search operation project was launched by the families of KAL 858 and their
supporters. In a nutshell, the family members, activists and supporters hurt
each other and split apart. What happened? It is a very complicated story.

The families have long been asking for a comprehensive reinvestigation
including a fresh search to locate the wreckage. The government's response
was far from the families' wishes. There had been two very limited reinvestigations by the government agencies so far, but no proper search operation
took place within these attempts. Following the apparently failed reinvestigations, the families kept working with no satisfactory results during the
two conservative governments. A positive sign emerged, however. When the
relatively liberal Moon Jae-in government was launched, a close cooperation
was established between the families and the authorities. The families now
exclusively focused on the launch of a fresh search. Several talks were held
and the families' expectations were high. Unfortunately, the negotiation could
not result in an actual search operation. That was why the families decided
to get this project done without the government's help. In other words, a
civilian-led search was actively considered and pursued.

This alternative plan came with several risks. One of the most sensitive
issues was concerned with money. The question of how to privately finance
the project was never simple. There were no easy answers. Indeed, it was
this financial question that made the families give up their previous attempt a
long time ago. Sadly, this same old question was raised again. A senior activist supporting the family members sketched out a plan along with expense
details. The plan was reviewed by a leading member of the family organisation. As part of this review process, the leading family member cross-checked
the project costs especially in relation to search equipment. It appeared that
there were more affordable options for the device. The leading family member subsequently discussed the matter with the senior activist. This issue then
evolved into something much bigger. A suspicion over personal financial
gains, time pressure and different opinions created the fundamental question
of trust among the related parties. Now the anger and hostility grew between
the senior activist and leading family member. I had known both sides quite

some time and they told me their own side of the story, blaming each other. I felt that they were becoming almost enemies.

After a few months, a third party who was involved in the reinvestigation campaigns contacted me. The message said that the families of KAL had formally separated from the senior activist. Although I had a sense that the situation was serious, I did not expect such a thing. It was so painful to digest the news. My heart was broken. But deep inside me, I had to admit that it was not entirely surprising. I was aware that there had been controversies surrounding the activist. This is a very uncomfortable issue that I have been avoiding for a while. He is a relatively well-known figure in civil society. He has been one of the key members who engineered the reinvestigation campaigns for the last fifteen years or so. More than that, it was actually this person who coordinated the campaigns mobilising people and resources across the family organisation and civil society. The family members and myself were really grateful to him.

Several years ago, when I visited Korea for fieldwork on the case, someone assisting the family members contacted me. I was invited to a meeting and heard that there was a problem with the senior activist. According to the conversation that I had, the style of the activist was rather self-righteous; in the campaign-related meetings, many important decisions were made almost unilaterally; the campaigns needed to be run in a collective and cooperative manner, but that was not the case under the senior activist's heavy influence. This someone also said that the family members had been informed of the situation, but they expressed full confidence in the senior activist.

Hearing the story troubled me, although it did not come as a complete surprise; I myself have experienced something problematic for the last few years. But I tried to understand the activist. By any standard, nobody can deny that he played a significant role in running and publicising the reinvestigation campaigns. He has organised almost every memorial ceremony since the early 2000s. He was devoted and energetic. That is how this activist gained trust from the family members. Full of plans, he has always remained a key figure throughout the campaigns.

On the other hand, he has had his own difficult moments. When he started to get involved in the campaigns, officials from the intelligence agency came to see him and gave a warning. And partly due to his activities, as he was a priest, he was asked by church authorities to go abroad and serve there for several years. But he just did not stop; he worked more actively and even collected the case-related materials during his leave. Upon his return to Korea, he kept working with the families and other supporters. People, myself included, really respected him. The problem seemed to become apparent in 2018, then rapidly got worse the following year. The period coincided with the active pursuit of the search project. He appeared to have been very frustrated with the government's slow response as time went by, which might have contributed to the problem.

Having been contacted by both sides, I decided to meet them all during my scheduled fieldwork in 2019. I planned to attend the memorial ceremony in November and expected to see them anyway. Apart from that, the activist wanted to see me personally, so I agreed to meet him because I had to figure out the problem more clearly. My heart was really heavy during the trip to Korea. In our meeting, the activist explained the situation in detail. I mainly listened and told him that I also planned to see the leading family member in question to cross-check the story. Then he asked me to convey his message to that person, if possible. The main message was that what had passed was past and he was ready to step away honourably. It appeared that while he wanted to reconcile, he did not want the problem to be discussed further among more family members.

Following the meeting, I did not know what to do. Should I deliver the message to that family member? My instinct said no. Most of all, I felt that I did not know the situation well enough to get involved. I also knew the difficult and complicated nature of reconciliation. But part of me said, 'Yes go ahead.' I was already in this complicated process in one way or another. Furthermore, I felt guilty because I had been away from both sides, away from Korea for a long time. So I thought delivering the message would be something good that I could do during my visit.

The aforementioned leading family member is a daughter of the former president of the family organisation. Her mother led the reinvestigation campaigns for about fifteen years and had to step down due to health issues. Following in the mother's footsteps, she has played an important role along with other active members.

I had worked with the former president for several years until I left Korea and maintained contact with her afterwards as well. When I visited Korea since then, I met the president (and her daughter) usually at a memorial ceremony or at her home. This time, I went to her house before the memorial ceremony to see her and her daughter. My main focus was on the meeting with the daughter, a current leading member of the family organisation. The leading member told me her side of the story and I was able to get to know more about the situation. At some point, she said that she did not record phone conversations with the senior activist, meaning there was no evidence. It was a bit awkward for me to hear such a thing, but I realised that she told me because she thought I would not believe her. That made me sad, because one of the reasons the families suffered for so long was that people just did not believe them. Of course, I believed her, but thinking of that moment still saddens me.

A much sadder and hugely tense moment came later on. Initially I decided, as mentioned, not to become a mediator between the two parties. But once I met the leading family member, I almost spontaneously changed my mind and delivered a message from the activist. As soon as I told her the message, she said in a cold voice. 'I never imagined that you came here to tell such a story. I thought you came to see my mother.' It became clear that she was surprised and disappointed. Her changed tone indicated that she was about to lose trust in me. Her facial expression also supported that premonition. She seemed to think that I was sent by the activist. To avoid any misunderstanding, I told her why I came in detail. Fortunately, she understood me. Thus, the short-lived credibility crisis ended without any significant harm. Or at least, that was my reading. It was really scary. The trust of more than ten years could have been gone in just one minute. I learnt a heavy lesson. You do not want to act as a mediator in such a hurry; a hasty intervention to bring reconciliation could backfire; and the word reconciliation should not be used lightly. Looking back, I was too naïve. I did not fully understand the gravity of the situation.

Indeed, the situation was much more serious than I thought. The family association would soon be split into two groups: the original organisation supporting the leading family member and a new organisation supporting the senior activist. More specifically, many family members left the organisation to establish their own group. The president of the original organisation was supposed to hand over the presidency to another person, but the complicated thing was that she supported the activist. She stepped down somehow reluctantly, then became a new president of the newly established family group. The family organisation was broken, so was my heart. It made me think harder about issues surrounding the senior activist. I have not personally challenged him, because I felt indebted to him for a long time, particularly since I had left Korea. After all, it was this activist who stayed and worked with the families. Having seen the gravely damaged family organisation, however, I now began to have mixed feelings more than ever.

This tragic development forced me to think about what it means to speak and act on behalf of other people. What does it mean to talk about the pain of others? What kinds of issues are there to consider? Why would you want to help other people? How could you help them? At what cost? And are there any gains?

These are difficult but necessary questions to ask. The activist's devotion and contribution have been significant in the reinvestigation campaigns. It is undeniable. But I suppose that he, at some point, might have begun to focus on the result rather than the process. The top priority was to get things done at any cost. Communications and negotiations with the family members and other supporters might not have been cherished enough. Given the grave consequences, I am not sure whether this problematic process was worthy enough. As such, the controversy surrounding the senior activist has raised uncomfortable questions. It also made me reflect on myself as a researcher. I wonder if I have otherised or objectified the families and their pain for my research. I wonder if I have treated the family members primarily only as objects of my research. I sincerely hope I have not.

Meanwhile, another dramatic development was made in early 2020. The potential wreckage of KAL 858 was detected in the Andaman Sea near Burma (Myanmar). Contrary to the official findings, the newly discovered objects were largely undamaged. The main body of the plane, or the fuselage and a portion of the wing structure were remarkably well-preserved. There was no guarantee that they actually belonged to KAL 858, because the observation was made only through an underwater camera. A high possibility was still reported. It was an immensely significant discovery.

Despite its significance, a cautious approach was needed. First of all, the search project was designed by a broadcasting company in cooperation with the aforementioned senior activist. Many of the family members were not consulted. Actually, the leading members of the family organisation had prepared for a separate search project with another broadcasting company. Secondly, the wreckage was detected in a controversial manner. In order to search that particular area, permission was needed from the Burmese government. A different company, supported by the family organisation, was in the process of getting this permission. But there was a delay, and the activist-friendly company conducted the search without formal permission. That was how they succeeded. Thirdly, the discovery was publicised in a way that the new family group gained legitimacy. The aforementioned broadcasting company needed some family members to run the story, but they did not want to work with the original family organisation. Hence the new group with support from the senior activist was invited to fill that gap; subsequently the original group was excluded from the relevant process.

For these reasons, I could not take the news about the potential wreckage with joy. It needs to be understood in the context of sad and complicated politics, along with ethical issues, surrounding the family organisation. To be fair, the search project in question was necessary and successful. The effort of the people involved should be valued. But the pain caused by this project cannot be ignored. This is a sensitive issue, and I have no definite answer at the moment.

Since the early 2000s I have attended memorial ceremonies whenever I could. The 2019 ceremony was exceptional in many ways. The leading family member told me in advance that the ceremony this time would be challenging and different. Up until 2018, almost every ceremony was planned and organised by the senior activist. As the conflict between the family members and the activist grew more and more, however, it was unclear whether the ceremony could take place at all. She said that the activist had all the information and materials regarding the annual ceremony and refused to hand them over to her and the other members. I did not know the exact situation, but that was what I heard. And I was ready to help; I used to help on the day of the ceremony anyway. The leading family member, a volunteer and I agreed to meet early in the morning of the day of the ceremony. Together, we set up things and so on.

Although the leading member was very worried, the ceremony went relatively smoothly. The most unique part, which had not been seen before, was that some family members shared their stories and the photos of their loved ones with participants. The members came forward one by one, standing next to a big screen where the photos appeared, and talked about their memories. This scene to me was quite symbolic, because unlike the previous ceremonies, it showed that the family members were at centre stage as main speakers. It was like a moving declaration saying that the families themselves were at the forefront of the reinvestigation campaigns.

The senior activist, who had organised previous ceremonies, also came. Understandably the atmosphere was a bit tense. The tension was heightened when the family organisation read out a statement. The vice-president made clear that the family organisation opposed any privately funded search projects; the organisation had been demanding the government-led search. In practice, that meant that the organisation would oppose a search project that was being planned by the senior activist. The statement section had always been part of the ceremony, but what was different in this case was that it publicly raised an issue about the activist, a long-term ally of the family organisation.

The tension reached its highest point when families had a general assembly after the ceremony. The senior activist read out his own statement and left. Then the family members had a heated discussion. Several people even shouted at each other. My observation was that many members were not happy with the senior activist. This sensitive discussion was followed by an election of new board members. The sitting president, who supported the senior activist, had earlier said that she would not continue her position for personal reasons. Accordingly, a new president and other board members were elected. They all had a similar position on the activist: they were critical of him.

As it stands now, the senior activist's words and actions need to be critically evaluated. But the thing is not so clear-cut. I am aware that he had wanted to step back. Sometime in 2005 he privately told me that he was considering staying away from the reinvestigation campaign. Because his role was so significant at the time, I replied that the campaign would not be able to be run without him. About thirteen years later I heard a similar thing. When I visited Korea for my fieldwork in 2018, I attended the memorial ceremony and met him. The activist wanted me to return to Korea and take over his role, or at least help him. I could feel that he was exhausted. I felt sorry for him. Then, the conflict became visible the following year and rapidly intensified. I cannot help but ask myself, what if he had stepped back in 2005? What if I had taken over his role in 2018?

The split itself was really hard to take in. What had confused me more was the name of the new organisation. It was called the Bereaved Families of KAL 858. When the very first family organisation was set up in the late 1980s, the leading family members largely accepted the government's official findings. The organisation's formal position was that the plane had been destroyed by North Korea and consequently 115 people were killed. At that time the organisation was also called the Bereaved Families because many families agreed with the government: the people on board were all dead. Therefore, demanding a full reinvestigation was not the families' priority.

This position changed in the early 2000s when the leading members of the organisation were replaced by the ones refusing to accept the official findings. The organisation's new position was that there were unanswered questions surrounding the case and thus the reinvestigation should have been launched. Indeed, for example the substantial wreckage such as the plane's black box was not detected and the bodies of 115 people were not recovered at all. But one thing was clear to the new leading members: the plane and people had disappeared. That was why the families began to call themselves the Families of the Missing People/Passengers. In other words, the term itself does matter.

Hence it was no wonder that I was very confused by the name of the splinter group: the Bereaved Families. Then does this group accept the government's findings? That is hardly the case. To my knowledge, they do demand the reinvestigation. The difference between this group and the Families of the Missing People is concerned with the search project. The members of the splinter group largely support the coordinator and his search plan. When the news broke in January 2020 that the privately funded project team, backed by the coordinator, had located the potential wreckage, the team and coordinator seemed to need the families' support and participation. But the then family organisation of the missing people was in conflict with the coordinator. That was how this splinter group was created. And a new organisation was required to have a new name. That is, the Bereaved Families, which implies that the significant wreckage is now found and the people on board are dead.

The tricky thing is that the object, at the time of writing (October 2021), has still not been confirmed as the wreckage of KAL 858. Of course there is a high probability that the wreckage belongs to KAL, but officially no confirmation has been made yet. Thus, the name of the splinter group demonstrates the immensely sensitive nature of the circumstances surrounding the families and the case in general.

The existence of two different family organisations has further complicated the development of the already-complex case. The current South Korean government has formed a task force team to identify the object. Both family organisations got involved in the process and sometimes the cleavage between the two negatively affected the negotiation. For instance, they disagreed over whether the families themselves should be dispatched to verify the object. Once it became clear that the families themselves would not participate in the dispatch team, they then had different opinions about which experts need to be nominated for the team. And when one candidate was rejected by another family group (and therefore by the government), this expert made strong complaints. The negotiation has never been smooth.

More broadly, the reinvestigation campaigns organised by both groups have sent confusing signals to other people. For example, several politicians were approached by the families. When they realised that there were two separate associations, they found themselves in a difficult situation. These politicians were willing to help the campaigns, but the question was whether to work with the original group or the splinter group. As such, the conflict within the families has clearly erupted since the discovery of the potential wreckage and the subsequent launch of the splinter group.

This problem, however, has not been widely visible in public for several reasons. As far as I know, the reinvestigation campaign supporters urged the families to form a united front. There has been a major concern that an image of divided families would harm the campaigns and the supporters of the official findings would take advantage of it. Also, some family members knew that if the conflict became public, it would eventually damage them. Of course it was undeniable that the families were divided. But partly for the above reasons, both organisations have tried not to make it known to the public.

The situation changed in late November 2020. It was related to one of the most important days for the families: the memorial ceremony. To the best of my knowledge, at first there was an attempt to hold a ceremony together. But this effort failed to materialise. Therefore, each group decided to organise a ceremony separately. This means that the conflict within the families would be made public. It seemed to me that more controversies and damage were inevitable. As I have worked with the families on both sides for many years, the idea of holding separate memorial ceremonies saddened me deeply.

During the course of events, I was contacted by both organisations. They invited me to participate in their own memorial ceremony. The original group first contacted me and said that it was decided to have separate events. I was still abroad, so I was asked whether I could send a message marking their ceremony. I answered yes. A few days later the splinter group contacted and asked me to come to their event. I said that I had not returned to Korea yet, and they did not ask further. I know them all and have been contacted by both sides on various issues even after the split. I have tried to respond to them as politely and equally as possible. I am not sure how many people were invited by both groups at the same time, but it was clear that other people including reporters would find it confusing. It was only a matter of time before this memorial ceremony could become the most controversial and complicated ceremony ever.

I have previously attended many ceremonies, and the saddest one so far was the ceremony in 2019 that was mentioned earlier. Or more precisely, the saddest part was the general assembly that took place after the memorial ceremony. It was right before the family members split up. As described, there were fierce debates over the senior activist's role. There can be serious disagreements within one organisation. It is not so strange. The problem would begin when a particular organisation splits up and each group competes for legitimacy. This kind of conflict is often accompanied by blaming counterparts and spreading misinformation. I have seen such ugly fights in other civil society groups. I feared that the families of KAL could go in that direction as well. Indeed, such behaviour had already been observed from my communications with both groups. I was deeply worried that the already-tense situation could explode in case the two separate ceremonies would be held. Eventually, for unknown reasons, the splinter group's plan was cancelled, so only one ceremony went ahead.

'This all started with you.' I had an issue with one person and wanted to talk about it cautiously and politely. In the course of the conversation that we had, the person told me this five-word-sentence. The sentence was short, but clear: it was my fault. What hurt me most was the term 'all.' I was the one to be blamed for everything; the person became completely immune from any responsibility. It meant that I should not have raised the issue in the first place; I should have put up with the situation that was unfair to me; I should have been quiet; the status-quo should have been maintained; but because I raised the issue, things got complicated; hence I should be blamed for all of this . . . I was shocked and hurt by this accusation. It felt like I had been struck by a 5-centimeter knife.

The word-knife is no stranger to me. This is where the case of KAL comes in again. It seems to me that I can now understand the case a bit better, yes a little bit better than before. The families of missing passengers had an issue with the government. They could not accept the official findings, because there were many unanswered questions, so they started reinvestigation campaigns. But the response was rather clear: the case was already over. From the government's point of view, the bomber had confessed to the crime and that was it; things were done long ago; do not make any trouble, let's just keep going; why do you make things complicated? Different situations, but similar logic. The status-quo was emphasised again. It could have been maintained by the silence of those families. The families, however, demanded a change or reinvestigation. That is how things got complicated, and this is those families' fault because they raised the issue. The government's reaction implies that the situation would have been stable as usual if the families had stayed quiet. The key message therefore is simple: 'This all started with you.'

Another thing I learnt from this message is something about isolation or loneliness. The person in question approached like-minded people and directly (and indirectly) used the mobilised power to pressure me to accept the above message. From their point of view, I was the problem: there was something wrong with me. I felt lonely and isolated.

This state of isolation reminded me, in a strange manner, of the case of KAL 858. At the beginning, those families who could not accept the official findings were marginalised. Initially the leading members of the family organisation largely accepted the government's investigation result. Their official priority was not to find answers to unresolved questions, but to move on for various reasons, which was to some extent understandable. This position was in line with the then strongly anti-North Korean military regime. It is therefore not surprising that the family organisation for some time maintained close relationships with the government and right-wing groups, all of which shared an anti-North Korean ideology. In this dominant framework, demands for a reinvestigation were discarded, or sometimes distorted as pro-North Korean voices (the families who had demanded the reinvestigation later became the leading members, and then the organisation as a whole managed to start the reinvestigation campaigns). Given my experience, I feel that I now see a bit better how lonely and isolated those families were.

In the course of this stressful event, part of my body was physically damaged. While I was using dental floss, I was thinking about the person who had accused me and how to deal with the situation. No matter how much I tried to understand, it was hard for me to accept the matter. It was unfair to me. Then suddenly, unpleasant and chilly feelings struck me. I stopped my hands, which had still been flossing, and realised that a little white thing was in the sink. At first, it looked like a food particle that was just removed from my teeth. Out of curiosity I decided to touch it. This white thing was hard, not like food. I immediately feared that something terrible had happened . . . Yes, it was my broken tooth. As I had not been focusing carefully enough on flossing, because I kept thinking about the person in question, I accidently broke my own tooth. I did not know what to do; I was just standing there for a while.

This incident has made me consider the notion of permanent damage. In a way, that person indirectly inflicted a tangible harm on me, which cannot be reversible. Now, whenever I eat, whenever I brush teeth, I can feel this broken part of my body. And this frequently reminds me of that person and the related unhappy event (I would later get expensive dental care, but I can still feel the damage that has been done).

The irreversible hurt leads to a different kind of harm. Things related to the cause of the damage would trigger a flashback. For instance, people with similar appearances or backgrounds to the person in question remind me of that very person. Going further, if these people exhibit similar characteristics or behaviour to that very person, the problem becomes more serious. This sort of chain reaction is complicated and uncomfortable. I struggle to keep going and stay positive. However, there is something inside me that makes me determined to prevent this from dictating my life. The seemingly unwanted attachment constitutes a stark difference to the 'this-all-started-with-you' narrative, a narrative of detachment. The speaker of this message, in particular by using the term 'all,' completely turned away from the event. In other words, the sole and whole responsibility of the event fell on me, the receiver of the same message. While the speaker disappeared from a complexly connected world, I am left alone with unwanted and continuous attachments. I wish I had that speaker's ability to detach. I wish I could forget everything.

Strangely but unsurprisingly, a familiar flight comes in once more. I remember one family member of KAL 858 who suddenly got nervous during the interview that we had. She lost her son because of this case and whenever she hears airplane sounds, she gets distressed. Yes, during our interview a plane flew over her house. I think I can now better understand her reaction back then. I also remember another family member who used to get sad whenever she saw young women. Her daughter had been a flight attendant aboard KAL 858. She said that those young women reminded her of the daughter she had lost. With my experience, I could reflect on this family member's words again.

But the most disturbing and hurtful thing was the way that accuser had looked at me. The person stared down at me as if I were a strange creature or trash. That mean stare . . . It was so cold. The person kept talking to me, but I could not hear because I was almost frozen. That stare was full of disrespect and disgust. My dignity was ripped out. This hurtful moment reminded me of what a family member of KAL once said: 'We were treated as less than bugs.' Their case was already closed long ago—the bomber confessed, the government investigated and the court upheld the official findings. These families, however, still wanted a reinvestigation. That was why they were treated as such—not less than human, but less than bugs. Until that stare hit me, I could not imagine what this feeling was like. But I think I now know a bit more about this feeling.

In addition, I realise that it has not been so difficult to find that stare elsewhere. I see this way of looking in white police officers—how they treated African Americans. I see this stare in imperial powers—how they treated colonised people. However, I might be exaggerating something here. And I do not regard myself as a completely innocent party. It might be the case that KAL 858 has made me more sensitive and empathetic towards pain and emotions. In any case, that way of looking raises a lot of questions. Those cold eyes, and that remarkably calm voice . . . '*I find no words / [. . .] for the scream / that wretches from my throat / it has no space / in your polite politics / in your rationalisms / of coloniality*' (Motta 2018: 16–17).

PART III

Destiny

Twenty years. Yes, I have followed the spy mystery for twenty years—I dealt with the case partly in my unofficial bachelor's thesis, then comprehensively in my master's thesis and more thoroughly and differently in my PhD thesis. Over the course of the investigation, a lot of dramatic events happened. Unhappy twists and turns. They pained me deeply. They suffocated me suddenly. At the same time, I have begun to believe that research on this case is my destiny. Whenever I was struggling to breathe, I thought, 'This is my destiny.' Whenever I was tempted to give up, I thought, 'This is my destiny.' Then surprisingly, I was empowered—'Yes, this is my destiny. This was meant to happen. And I am meant to endure this.' It is not about overcoming something. Rather, this is about living with it, enduring it—a mysterious power that allows me to go until the end. I actually think that there is no fixed or fully closed *end* in any events/cases (things are always in-the-making). But the point is to finish your marathon, to run, walk or crawl until the end, regardless of the result.

Especially for the last few years, something distressing has continued. Everything I planned, everything I wrote, did not go well; they are all related to the case of KAL 858 in one way or another. More specifically, those plans and writings could have been finished earlier, but the relevant process has been delayed in almost every case. A prolonged wait, without enough, if any, explanations. I might have missed something. There must be some understandable reasons. Those uncertainties have made me feel demotivated. Looking back, this is nothing new. I have had similar experiences before (in and beyond academia). I suppose other people would experience this kind of thing at some point. Apart from that, I am aware that sometimes things can just happen. They are beyond our plans and control. When our circumstances are not favourable, we cannot do things even if we want to. Life is not simple, not so linear.

Another thing is that during my years of research on this mysterious and controversial bombing case, I have witnessed the families of victims going through a similar but much more serious delay—waiting for answers from the government and other related parties (this is not unique to this case if you think about numerous victims of state violence or human rights abuses demanding apologies/explanations over decades). Of course, there are differences between this state-related matter and my story of delay. The focus here is on what it is like to be left waiting without enough information.

All those experiences made me think that I would not let other people face such things, at least on my part. For example, I always try to respond to students' inquiries at my earliest convenience. If questions require some time to consider, I tell people that I will get back to them by a specific date/time so that they can have some (tangible) picture of the proceedings. If I cannot keep a promise, I offer apologies with explanations. Whether it is about emails, grading or something else, I almost always, and sincerely, try. I learnt it from lived experience. It is embedded in my body—a small piece of my destiny, unexpectedly but mysteriously associated with KAL 858.

But still, yes still, I have to confess: Part of me wants to escape from KAL 858, whilst part of me equally wants to fly further. The plane that disappeared keeps flying around me. It keeps coming back to me. It keeps hurting me. But a mysterious narrative of destiny keeps saving me. It might be possible that I am comfortable with the word destiny partly because of my Korean/Asian background. Yet, ironically I have been inspired, or my initial idea of destiny has been reinforced, by non-Asian movies and dramas. For instance, *The Lord of the Rings*—Frodo, a young hobbit from J. R. R. Tolkien's fiction, is heavily burdened with his unexpected task but manages to carry on until the end. Or *Conviction*—Betty, a working mother drawn from an actual event, decides to attend law school and become a lawyer only because she wants to prove her brother's innocence in a murder case. Frodo and Betty, if I have not told you before, 'Thank you.'

Once I started to regard difficult moments as part of my destiny related to the case, mysteriously I felt relieved. 'This was meant to happen, and I am meant to endure it . . . ' I decided to believe in the power of destiny. I decided to become a cautious optimist. In other words, I tried to formulate a narrative that would actively interpret my difficulty and suffering to support or save me. Apparently, the key theme here was destiny. It allowed me to interpret the difficult moments from a long-term perspective. Molly Andrews (2007: 11) suggests that one could reconstruct events as a different kind of story, once they are placed within a wider temporal approach. To me, the destiny-narrative made it possible to interpret my difficult moments as one piece of a lifetime puzzle. It gave me some space to breathe when I was unable to breathe. It made me realise that every step, every moment of ups and downs, could mean something—everything is related, whether positive or negative. They are, or can be, parts of my work, my writing and my life.

Detectives

Like many other tragic events, the case of KAL 858 should not have happened in the first place. It has led to various forms of unfortunate matters. One such example is the conflict among family members. If the case itself is a tragedy, this conflict can be called a tragedy within a tragedy. And I have also become trapped in this tragedy, even though I did not intend to. It is concerned with the potential wreckage of the plane discovered in the Andaman Sea, as mentioned before, in early 2020. Two different family organisations have had talks with the government to confirm whether the wreckage belongs to KAL 858. Each organisation nominated a representative for the search team. To cut a long story short, I have been nominated as a third-party representative not attached to either family organisation. This was a rather unexpected move.

I have long been waiting for the second-term TRC to be launched in South Korea. As the first-term Commission's attempt to reinvestigate the case failed, there was a possibility that a new Commission would investigate the case again. When the relevant legislative process was finalised after a long delay, I decided to return to Korea temporarily. That was partly because people had asked me to come to Korea. Moreover, based on my research and expertise on the case of KAL 858, I wanted to make a very specific and tangible contribution.

Before my arrival in December 2020, the search team was already organised so I did not think that I could participate in the team. Once I arrived in Korea, however, I was asked whether I would be interested in participating in the search operation. As far as I know, the government aimed to dispatch the team in November 2020, but the plan did not materialise. The awkward circumstances ironically gave me an opportunity. Indeed, as a researcher I would be able to actually contribute to the investigation. A new operation was scheduled to take place in February 2021. Hence I agreed to join the team quite unexpectedly and willingly. But it was not so simple. The family organisation and its splinter group have been in conflict since the official break-up of the family members in early 2020. The nomination had to be approved by both sides.

The problem was that the splinter group believed that I had sided with the original group. So they indirectly, not directly, opposed the nomination. Being aware of the issue, I contacted and met the president of the splinter group. We had a conversation for several hours and the result was positive. Things looked okay. Now I began to actively prepare for the search operation. I even started to learn Burmese. Then I felt something was wrong. I was supposed to get further information on the search but received no news. It turned out that the splinter group's position had somewhat changed. It was a shock.

I told the person in charge that if the splinter group was not happy with my participation, then I would not join the team. My goal was not to join this operation by whatever means. I did want to be part of the reinvestigation process in one way or another, but never wanted to be a burden for any family members. The person in charge respected my wish, but I was told that there would still be a possibility and a formal discussion would be held. So I waited, but the result was negative: my participation was nullified. To be honest, I was deeply hurt and disappointed. With this scandal, I realised that the situation surrounding the conflict among the family members was much more serious than I had thought. The scandal indicated that my words and actions would be interpreted quite differently by the concerned parties regardless of my sincerity and caution. On a separate note, the search operation was again postponed abruptly due to the military coup in Burma. It was just before the dispatch of the search team—the timing could not have been more dramatic. Apart from my cancelled participation, another delay in the operation really saddened me.

With the wound from the above scandal, I got confused and felt powerless. Those families had worked together to achieve one same goal until not long ago. I know it because I myself had worked with them. Now, they are enemies. I do not have to, and will not, take any side in verifying the wreckage. If it belongs to KAL 858, that would be great. If it does not belong to KAL 858, that would be disappointing. That is all. Nothing less, nothing more—I or anyone else in the search team does not need to, and cannot, lie. The operation will be recorded and documented. This is not about taking someone's side. But in the families' views, you are already framed in a certain manner. There is no place for agency, devotion or faith. The system of distrust and confrontation would overrule any good-heartedness. Another tragedy within the tragedy, I would say.

Trapped in the conflict among the family members, there was still something that could be done. Sticking to my original plan, I could apply for a position at the TRC. In this case, there is no need to be nominated by someone; the application does not need to be approved by the families of KAL 858. What troubled me was that I had made several applications for the similar position fifteen years before and failed each time. Yes, as mentioned earlier, I applied to become an investigator when the first-term Commission was established. People around me said that my qualification would be enough to join the Commission. But I failed. This time, people said again that I could become an investigator. I myself also believed that there was a strong possibility of me joining the Commission—I have now earned a PhD degree and acquired more experience. Still, my biggest worry was related to lack of actual investigation experience. There have been several investigative government agencies, the first-term Commission included, where civilians worked as investigators. It was expected that many of those people would apply for the positions at the newly-launched Commission. In other words, I was supposed to compete with the highly experienced former investigators as applicants. Would I have a possibility in this process?

To address that question, I took a creative but risky approach: I decided to talk about my previous failure in the Statement of Purpose.

Fifteen years ago, I applied to become an investigator at the first-term TRC. The result was not good. This year, I write the application again. Over the last fifteen years, my desire to join the TRC, and my hope to contribute to transitional justice towards making a better future, have not changed. With this in mind, let me introduce myself as follows.

The reason why I became interested in the TRC and transitional justice is related to something that happened when I was a university student. I participated in a thesis competition organised by the Ministry of Unification. Thankfully, I won the second prize. A few days before the award ceremony, however, I was told that I needed to revise my thesis. Defending academic freedom and freedom of conscience, I refused to yield to the demand. The problem was concerned with a particular case, a so-called historical issue. It occurred in the late 1980s and despite the government's official findings, various questions have been raised. That was why I suggested that the case needed to be reinvestigated. The government stated that this case was already closed with the Supreme Court's verdict; consequently, my award was cancelled. I was hurt, and consumed with confusion. Thanks to this scandal though, I became involved in transitional justice campaigns.

The first-term TRC was established in 2005 when the relevant law was passed. I was not a professional activist, but as a researcher I worked with human rights activists and victims of state violence to pass the law. Around the time when the TRC was launched, I wrote an MA thesis about the aforementioned past issue. My acquaintances encouraged me to apply for a position at the TRC. I was planning to go abroad to do a PhD. After careful consideration, I changed my mind and applied to the TRC. But I failed to become an investigator (several times). It was a huge disappointment. This frustration led me to decide to become an *unofficial* investigator. Now as an independent detective, I researched that past issue and earned a PhD degree. My work on transitional justice continued even after the PhD. And today, I am applying for a position at the TRC again.

My related experiences include [. . .].

Importantly, I conceptualised my failure as a strong sense of duty as a potential investigator: 'Although I do not know exactly, it can be safely said that many people with a background in the first-term Commission or other agencies may have applied. But I am sure that there are not many people like me who had failed before, then wanted to apply again this year. It proves how sincere I am—this shows my strong sense of duty.' I passed a document screening and got an invitation to interview. I made a list of some potential interview questions in the course of preparation. Among them was the question about practical experience in investigation. I was right. This question did come up. In my answer, I tried to highlight the similarities between (academic) research and (practical) investigation: collecting information or evidence, analysing materials, interviewing, writing reports and so on. Indeed, IR scholars such as Robert O. Koehane (1988) and James Der Derian (2009) used to identify a researcher as a detective. Including this question, at least from my point of view, the interview as a whole went relatively well.

I was relieved. Yes, everything seemed to go well. But more importantly, I felt comfortable because I had a dream about a pig. There is a saying in Korea that if pigs appear in your dream, that is a sign of good luck. I have rarely had such a dream in my life. On the interview day, however, I woke up from this precious pig dream. So I was quite sure that the result of my application would be positive. I was fully ready to become a researcher-detective. Had my dream actually turned into a dream job? It turned into a shock: I failed . . . Yes, I could not find my name on the list of successful candidates. 'Is it a bad dream?' I wondered. Unfortunately, it was not a dream. I did fail. Once I realised it, I went weak at the knees. I suddenly felt exhausted. I was speechless.

What should I do? I was certain that it was the right decision to come to Korea to submit the application. As a researcher, I wanted to make a real impact beyond a scholarly community. But more importantly, I wanted to accommodate the families' wishes. It would have been more convenient for me to stay in Europe; I would still have done something, for example through writing or online activities.

In the course of returning to Korea, almost everything was more complicated and stressful in the age of COVID-19: paperwork, parcel delivery, self-quarantine for two weeks and various additional costs related to the move. Furthermore, I had to struggle with South Korea's everyday disaster, the issue that I have not dealt with in Europe: a growing fine dust problem. You would need to wear a mask in Korea not only because of the pandemic, but also because of poor air quality (especially in the winter and spring). It is not even recommended to go outside when the dust problem becomes serious.

Finland has the cleanest air in the world, meaning that as a person who likes to take a walk regularly, it was difficult for me to adapt to a new environment.

I knew that all these problems, together with the pandemic, would make my temporary life in Korea depressing. But I chose to embrace the problems because it would pay off. I now began to regret my decision. It was not an exaggeration. The participation in the search team had been scrapped due to the conflict among the family members. Then the application to become an official investigator had collapsed for some reason. All doors seemed to be closed.

I asked myself: What went wrong? Am I too ambitious as a researcher? Should I have remained in Europe? Why is it difficult for me to let go of KAL 858? Am I too much devoted? Or obsessed? Where is the line between devotion and obsession? I have seriously challenged myself for about two weeks. Upon my arrival in Korea, I had to self-isolate for two weeks due to coronavirus restrictions. This time, I faced another kind of self-isolation. It was a lonely and dark moment. When this isolation ended, coincidently, the TRC issued an additional recruitment announcement. After a short hesitation, I read it somewhat reluctantly. To my surprise, my heart began to pound . . . again. I had a lot of mixed emotions.

Do I still want to become a researcher-detective? 'Yes,' I said to myself. So I applied again, but failed. Another recruitment was announced later. Without hesitation I applied again. The interview went well. I was quite sure that I would be able to make it this time. Although I have no particular religion, I prayed a lot . . . Maybe my prayers were not enough. I failed again. Yes, *again* . . .

With the three consecutive failures, I was in deep frustration. It felt that I had done enough. Actually, it might be better not to join the TRC. Even if I become an investigator, there is no guarantee that *I* could investigate the case of KAL 858. It would be up to the TRC leadership to decide. Furthermore, I could even be advised to stay away from the case because the leadership might think that, as a researcher on this very case, I have some prejudice. Indeed, this question was raised within an earlier TRC-like body, where several investigators were excluded from investigations due to conflicts of interest or potential biases. Apart from that, like the first-term TRC, the current organisation has various limitations as a temporary commission in terms of resources, investigative powers and operational period. In addition, if I become an investigator, hence a civil servant, I would not be able to write and speak about the case freely during and after the TRC work.

Taken all together, it would be wise to remain outside the Commission. So I decided not to apply anymore. Instead, I began planning to file a FOIA request to the TRC. For what purpose? To find out why I had continuously failed to get the position there. I wanted to see all the materials in relation to the assessment of my applications. Just to make sure, I called the TRC and asked. 'In this selection, there are some people who did not make it. Is that because they did not do well in the interviews?' 'Yes.'

As soon as I heard it, that short and cold answer, I realised that I was not ready to give up: I could not admit that I had done the interview terribly. I could not accept that I was not suitable to become an investigator. Thus, when a new recruitment was announced, I applied. Shortly after this application, the TRC announced another recruitment. I again applied. Interestingly, the results of both recruitments were scheduled to be released on the same day. Regardless of the results, there would be no further applications, I thought. Yes, this would be the last . . . I was determined. Finally, the day came. I checked out the result of my fourth application. I had failed. I was not surprised. Then the result of my fifth application, the last one. I took a deep breath. Before checking out the result, I almost covered my eyes as if I was watching a horror film. Then slowly, very slowly . . . I began to peek through my fingers.

Bibliography

Andrews, Molly. (2007). *Shaping History: Narratives of Political Change*. Cambridge, UK: Cambridge University Press.

Barry, Lynda. (2008). *What It Is*. Montreal: Drawn & Quarterly.

Binet, Laurent. (2013). *HHhH*. London: Vintage.

Cho, Hongmin. (2011). 'Pyoungil Kim "Sad" Hyunhee Kim "Glad" About Kim Jong-il.' *Kyunghyang Shinmun*, 24 December (in Korean).

Coelho, Paulo. (2003). *The Alchemist*. San Francisco, CA: HarperOne.

Der Derian, James. (2009). *Virtuous War: Mapping the Military-Industrial-Media-Entertainment Network*, 2nd ed. New York and London: Routledge.

DFAT (Department of Foreign Affairs and Trade). (1988). 'KAL CRASH.' 15 January.

E-News. (2010). 'Distrust of the "Investigation of Cheonan" Is Spreading.' *Hankyoreh*, 8 September (in Korean).

Enloe, Cynthia. (1989). *Bananas, Beaches and Bases: Making Feminist Sense of International Politics*. London: Pandora.

Keohane, Robert O. (1998). 'Beyond Dichotomy: Conversations Between International Relations and Feminist Theory.' *International Studies Quarterly*, 42(1), 193–98.

KCNA (Korean Central News Agency). (2011). 'Kim Jong Il Passes Away (Urgent).' 19 December (in Korean).

Lee, Yoojin. (2013). 'Always Kept Under Surveillance by the National Intelligence Service.' *Hankyoreh*, 29 April (in Korean).

MBC. (2013). 'MBC Special Interview: Mayumi's Life, Hyunhee Kim's Confession.' 15 January (in Korean).

Motta, Sara C. (2018). *Liminal Subjects: Weaving (Our) Liberation*. London: Rowman & Littlefield International.

News Y. (2014). 'Yul Shin's Jungjungdangdang.' 17 March (in Korean).

Nocut TV. (2009). 'Hyunhee Kim "I Am Not a Fake".' 11 March (in Korean).

Park-Kang, Sungju. (2014). *Fictional International Relations: Gender, Pain and Truth*. London: Routledge.

SBS. (2010). 'Hyunhee Kim's Visit to Japan With Non-significant Results.' 24 July (in Korean).

Strausz, Erzsébet. (2018). *Writing the Self and Transforming Knowledge in International Relations*. London: Routledge.

Thies, Cameron G. (2002). 'A Pragmatic Guide to Qualitative Historical Analysis in the Study of International Relations.' *International Studies Perspective*, 3(4), 351–72.

TRC (Truth and Reconciliation Commission). (2008a). 'KAL 858 Archives.' DA0799647 (in Korean).

TRC (Truth and Reconciliation Commission). (2008b). 'KAL 858 Archives.' DA0799649 (in Korean).

TRC (Truth and Reconciliation Commission). (2008c). 'KAL 858 Archives.' DA0799644 (in Korean).

TV Chosun. (2012). 'The Current Affairs Talk Show Pan.' 18 June (in Korean).

U.S. GPO (Government Printing Office). (1989). 'The Bombing of Korean Airlines Flight KAL-858: Hearing and Markup.' Committee on Foreign Affairs.

Vuong, Ocean. (2017). *Night Sky wiith Exit Wounds*. London: Jonathan Cape.

YTN. (2015). 'Joonsuk Ho's News In.' 27 November (in Korean).

Index

Ingram Content Group UK Ltd.
Milton Keynes UK
UKHW012043100523
421545UK00002B/14